THE OXFORD HANDBOO

ISLAMIC PHILOSOPHY

THE OXFORD HANDBOOK OF

ISLAMIC PHILOSOPHY

Edited by
KHALED EL-ROUAYHEB
and
SABINE SCHMIDTKE

OXFORD
UNIVERSITY PRESS

OXFORD
UNIVERSITY PRESS

Oxford University Press is a department of the University of Oxford. It furthers the University's objective of excellence in research, scholarship, and education by publishing worldwide. Oxford is a registered trade mark of Oxford University Press in the UK and certain other countries.

Published in the United States of America by Oxford University Press
198 Madison Avenue, New York, NY 10016, United States of America.

First issued as an Oxford University Press paperback, 2019

Library of Congress Cataloging-in-Publication Data
Names: El-Rouayheb, Khaled, editor.
Title: The Oxford handbook of Islamic philosophy / edited by Khaled El-Rouayheb and Sabine Schmidtke.
Description: New York, NY: Oxford University Press, 2016. | Series: Oxford handbooks | Includes index.
Identifiers: LCCN 2016002201 | ISBN 9780199917389 (hardcover: alk. paper) |
ISBN 9780190070076 (paperback: alk. paper)
Subjects: LCSH: Islamic philosophy.
Classification: LCC B741.O94 2016 | DDC 181/.07—dc23
LC record available at http://lccn.loc.gov/2016002201

Contents

Contributors

Peter Adamson is Professor of Late Ancient and Arabic Philosophy at the Ludwig-Maximilians-Universität in Munich. He is the author of *Al-Kindī* (Oxford University Press, 2007) and the editor of numerous books on philosophy in the Islamic world, including *Interpreting Avicenna: Critical Essays* (Cambridge University Press, 2013). He is also the author of a book series entitled A History of Philosophy Without Any Gaps, appearing with Oxford University Press.

Saleh J. Agha is a Lecturer at the Department of Philosophy at the American University of Beirut and Senior Editor at the *Mideast Mirror*. His main areas of interest are Wittgenstein, philosophical logic, and ancient Greek philosophy. He has been a Fulbright Scholar at Princeton University and Visiting Professor at Columbia University.

Asad Q. Ahmed is Associate Professor of Arabic and Islamic Studies in the Department of Near Eastern Studies, the University of California, Berkeley. His works include *The Religious Elite of the Early Islamic Ḥijāz* and *Avicenna's Deliverance: Logic.*

Khalil Andani is a doctoral student in Islamic Studies at Harvard University, where he focuses on Islamic theology and philosophy, Shīʿī Islam, and Ismāʿīlī history and thought. He holds a master of theological studies degree from Harvard Divinity School, and his prior publications include "The Metaphysics of the Common Word: A Dialogue of Eckhartian and Ismaili Gnosis" in *Sacred Web*, volumes 26 and 27.

Ahab Bdaiwi is Assistant Professor in Medieval Arabic Philosophy, Leiden University. His area of research is medieval and early modern Islamic intellectual history. He examines Avicennan philosophy and its reception in Shīʿī and Sunnī circles and intellectual milieus in medieval Iran and Iraq. He is the author of the forthcoming monograph *Shiʿi Defenders of Avicenna: An Intellectual History of the Philosophers of Shiraz.*

Catarina Belo is Associate Professor of Philosophy at the American University in Cairo, Egypt. She specializes in medieval Islamic philosophy and more recently in Aquinas and Hegel. She is the author of *Chance and Determinism in Avicenna and Averroes* (Brill, 2007) and *Averroes and Hegel on Philosophy and Religion* (Ashgate, 2013).

Amos Bertolacci (PhD in Philosophy, University of Florence, and in Near Eastern Languages and Civilization, Yale University) is Associate Professor of History of Islamic Philosophy at the Scuola Normale Superiore (Pisa, Italy). He is the author of *The Reception of Aristotle's Metaphysics in Avicenna's Kitāb al-Šifāʾ: A Milestone of Western*

Metaphysical Thought (Brill, 2006), and of an Italian annotated translation of the metaphysics of Avicenna's *Shifāʾ* (UTET, 2007).

Cécile Bonmarriage is *Chercheur qualifié* at the Fonds de la Recherche Scientifique (FRS-FNRS, Belgium) and Associate Professor at UCLouvain (Louvain-la-Neuve). Her research focuses on postclassical Islamic philosophy, with a special interest in the transformation of the Avicennan heritage in later Islamic thought.

Cristina D'Ancona is Professor of Philosophy at the Università di Pisa (history of philosophy in late Antiquity, Arabic philosophy, medieval philosophy). She is the author of *Recherches sur le Liber de Causis* (1995) and the author/editor of *Storia della filosofia nell'Islam medievale* (2005). Her book *La casa della sapienza: La trasmissione della filosofia greca e la formazione della filosofia araba* has been translated into Arabic (2014).

Alnoor Dhanani specializes in Islamic intellectual history, in particular the interaction between science, theology, and philosophy. He was educated at Columbia University in New York, McGill University, and Harvard University, where he obtained his PhD degree in 1991. He has been a Fellow at the Center for Middle Eastern Studies at Harvard University, a tutor in the Department of the History of Science and the Department for the Study of Religion at Harvard University, and a Visiting Lecturer at the Department of Comparative Religion at Tufts University. He is the author of *The Physical Theory of Kalam: Atoms, Space, and Void in Basrian Mu'tazili Cosmology.*

Khaled El-Rouayheb is Jewett Professor of Arabic and of Islamic Intellectual History at Harvard University. His research focuses on Islamic intellectual history, especially in the early modern period, and the history of Arabic logic. He is the author of *Relational Syllogisms and the History of Arabic Logic, 900–1900* (Brill, 2010) and *Islamic Intellectual History in the Seventeenth Century* (Cambridge University Press, 2015).

Fatemeh Fana is Associate Professor and Director of the Department of Philosophy at the Research Center of the Humanities (Encyclopaedia Islamica Foundation) in Tehran, Iran. She is the author of numerous articles on philosophical concepts in the *Encyclopaedia of the World of Islam* and on the metaphysics of Avicenna and Sabzawārī, and has written comparative studies on Avicenna and Saint Thomas Aquinas. She has also edited Alīqulī Khān's *Iḥyā-yi Ḥikmat* (*The Revival of Philosophy*), a work of Islamic philosophy from the eleventh/seventeenth century (published in Tehran, 1377/1988), and Khwāja Naṣīr al-Dīn Ṭūsī's *Risāla i'tiqādiyya (An Essay on Faith)* (published in Tehran, 1379/2000).

Emma Gannagé is Associate Professor at Georgetown University and editor of the *Mélanges de l'Université Saint-Joseph*. Her research interests include Greco-Arabic and Islamic philosophy. Among her most recent publications are "Al-Kindī, Ptolemy (and Nicomachus of Gerasa) Revisited," in *Philosophy in Islamic Lands*, edited by Th. A. Druart, and "Between Medicine and Natural Philosophy: Avicenna on Properties (*khawāṣṣ*) and Qualities (*kayfiyyāt*)," in *The Occult Sciences in Pre-Modern Islamic Culture*, edited by N. al-Bizri and E. Orthman.

Frank Griffel is Professor of Islamic Studies at Yale University. He is the author of numerous articles on Islamic theology and philosophy. In 2009 he published *Al-Ghazālī's Philosophical Theology* (Oxford University Press) and in 2000 *Apostasie und Toleranz im Islam* (Brill). He is a translator of al-Ghazālī and Averroes and the editor of three collective volumes on Islamic thought.

Sidney H. Griffith is Ordinary Professor Emeritus in the Department of Semitic and Egyptian Languages and Literatures in the Catholic University of America. His principal areas of research and writing are Syriac Patristics, Christian Arabic, and the history of Muslim/Christian interactions in early Islamic times. His works include a translation and edition of Yaḥyā ibn 'Adī's *The Reformation of Character* (2002), as well as the monographs *The Church in the Shadow of the Mosque* (2008) and *The Bible in Arabic* (2013).

Damien Janos is Ussher Assistant Professor of Classical Islamic Thought and Dialogue at Trinity College Dublin. He has worked for several years as a postdoctoral researcher in Germany (Ruhr University, University of Göttingen, Max Planck Institute for the History of Science) and is presently an independent scholar. His research focuses mainly on the philosophical works of al-Fārābī and Avicenna, with a secondary interest in the history of Arabic astronomy and astrology. He has recently edited a volume on Arabic Christian philosophy (*Ideas in Motion in Baghdad and Beyond: Philosophical and Theological Exchanges between Christians and Muslims in the Third/Ninth and Fourth/Tenth Centuries*, Brill, 2015).

Muhammad Ali Khalidi is Professor of Philosophy at York University in Toronto, specializing mainly in the philosophy of science and philosophy of mind. His book *Natural Categories and Human Kinds* (Cambridge University Press, 2013) discusses classification in the natural and social sciences. He also has research interests in classical Islamic philosophy and has published an anthology of translations from that tradition, *Medieval Islamic Philosophical Writings* (Cambridge University Press, 2005).

Taneli Kukkonen is Professor of Philosophy at New York University Abu Dhabi. He is the author of *Ibn Tufayl* (Oneworld, 2014) and over thirty research articles and book chapters on Arabic philosophy and the Aristotelian and Platonic traditions.

Jon McGinnis is Professor of Classical and Medieval Philosophy at the University of Missouri, St. Louis. In addition to numerous articles, he is the author of *Avicenna* in the Oxford University Press's Great Medieval Thinkers Series (2010), translator and editor of Avicenna's *Physics* from his encyclopedic work *The Healing* (Brigham Young University Press, 2009), and cotranslator with David C. Reisman of *Classical Arabic Philosophy: An Anthology of Sources* (Hackett , 2007).

Mustansir Mir teaches Islamic studies at Youngstown State University, Youngstown, Ohio. His main research interests are Qur'ānic studies and Iqbal studies. He is the author of *Understanding the Islamic Scripture* and *Iqbal.*

Nazif Muhtaroğlu is currently a Research Fellow at Boğaziçi University (Istanbul). He received his PhD from the Department of Philosophy at the University of Kentucky. He is the founder of the International Society for the Study of Occasionalism. He has edited *Classic Issues in Islamic Philosophy and Theology Today* (Springer, 2010) with Anna-Teresa Tymieniecka, and *The Logos of Life and Cultural Interlacing* (Springer, 2014) with A.-T. Tymieniecka and Detlev Quintern.

Reza Pourjavady is Hafis Visiting Lecturer for Religion and Culture of Iran at Goethe Universität, Frankfurt. His works include the monographs *Philosophy in Early Safavid Iran: Najm al-Dīn Maḥmūd al-Nayrīzī and His Writings* (Brill, 2011) and, coauthored with Sabine Schmidtke, *A Jewish Philosopher of Baghdad: 'Izz al-Dawla Ibn Kammūna (d.683/1284) and His Writings* (Brill, 2006).

Sajjad H. Rizvi is Associate Professor of Islamic Intellectual History and Director of the Institute of Arab and Islamic Studies at the University of Exeter. He specializes in the Safavid-Mughal period and is the author of *Mulla Sadra and Metaphysics* (Routledge, 2009). He is currently finishing a short monograph on Mir Damad and a comparative study of philosophy in eighteenth-century Iran and North India.

Sabine Schmidtke is Professor of Islamic Intellectual History at the Institute for Advanced Study, Princeton, NJ. Her works include numerous articles and editions, as well as monographs such as *The Theology of al-'Allāma al-Ḥillī* (1991), *Theologie, Philosophie und Mystik im zwölferschiitischen Islam des 9./15. Jahrhunderts: Die Gedankenwelten des Ibn Abī Ǧumhūr al-Aḥsā'ī (um 838/1434-35–nach 905/1501)* (Brill, 2000), and, coauthored with Reza Pourjavady, *A Jewish Philosopher of Baghdad: 'Izz al-Dawla Ibn Kammūna (d.683/1284) and His Writings* (Brill, 2006).

Ayman Shihadeh, DPhil, Oxford, is based at SOAS, University of London. He has published widely on the history of medieval Arabic philosophy and Islamic theology, including *The Teleological Ethics of Fakhr al-Dīn al-Rāzī* (Brill, 2006) and *Doubts on Avicenna: A Study and Edition of Sharaf al-Dīn al-Mas'ūdī's Commentary on the* Ishārāt (Brill, 2015). He serves as the Section Editor for Philosophy and Theology at the *Encyclopaedia of Islam*.

Tony Street is Assistant Director of Research in Islamic Studies at the Faculty of Divinity, Cambridge, and a Fellow of Clare Hall College. He works on medieval Islamic intellectual history.

Sarah Stroumsa is the Alice and Jack Ormut Professor Emerita of Arabic Studies, Hebrew University of Jerusalem. Among her published works in English are *Freethinkers of Medieval Islam: Ibn al-Rawandi, Abu Bakr al-Razi, and Their Impact on Islamic Thought* (Brill, 1999); *Maimonides in His World: Portrait of a Mediterranean Thinker* (Princeton University Press, 2010; paperback edition 2012), and Dawud al-Muqammas, *Twenty Chapters* (Brigham Young University Press, 2016).

John Walbridge received his BA from Yale University and his PhD from Harvard University in Near Eastern languages. He has taught in the Department of Near Eastern Languages and Cultures at Indiana University, Bloomington, since 1993. He is the author of three books on Suhrawardī and the Illuminationist school, and is the coauthor of the edition and translation of Suhrawardī's *The Philosophy of Illumination.* His most recent books are *God and Logic in Islam: The Caliphate of Reason* and *The Alexandrian Epitomes of Galen,* volume 1.

INTRODUCTION

KHALED EL-ROUAYHEB AND SABINE SCHMIDTKE

THE study of Islamic philosophy has entered a new and exciting phase in the last few years. Both the received canon of Islamic philosophers and the narrative of the course of Islamic philosophy are in the process of being radically questioned and revised. The bulk of twentieth-century Western scholarship on Arabic or Islamic philosophy focused on the period from the ninth century to the twelfth. It is a measure of the transformation that is currently underway in the field that the present *Oxford Handbook* has striven to give roughly equal weight to every century from the ninth to the twentieth.

I.1. Rethinking the Course of Islamic Philosophy

Older assumptions about the study of Islamic philosophy were part of a grand narrative according to which the Islamic world preserved and interpreted the Greek philosophical heritage during the European "Dark Ages" and later handed over this heritage to the Latin West in the course of the twelfth and thirteenth centuries. At this point, the role of the Islamic world in the narrative was over, and little scholarly attention was given to later Islamic philosophy. Some even speculated that, due to the disapproval of orthodox theologians, the philosophical tradition died out in the Islamic world in the twelfth century—so that, by a stroke of luck, the Latin West managed to take over the Greek philosophical heritage just in time, before the Islamic world itself repudiated this heritage and sank into fideist darkness. (Influential and older studies in this tradition include De Boer 1901; O'Leary 1922; Madkour 1934; Fākhūrī and Jurr 1957; Watt 1962.)

Three pioneering figures who questioned this narrative in the West starting from the 1960s were Henry Corbin, Seyyed Hossein Nasr, and Nicholas Rescher. Corbin and Nasr, influenced by a very different narrative of the history of Islamic philosophy that has survived in Iran, showed in a series of studies that the Islamic philosophical tradition continued without interruption in Shīʿī Iranian circles down to the modern period (see, for example, Corbin 1964; Nasr 1961, 1964). They emphasized in particular the rise of the anti-Peripatetic Platonist "Illuminationist" (*ishrāqī*) school of Suhrawardī (d. 587/1191) and the later synthesis of Illuminationist and mystical philosophy in seventeenth-century Iran. Rescher, for his part, drew attention to the continued vigor and sophistication of Arabic works on logic in the thirteenth century, a century after the supposed demise of the Islamic philosophical tradition (Rescher 1964, 1967).

The insights of Corbin, Nasr, and Rescher have since been incorporated into mainstream presentations of Islamic philosophy. The excellent *Cambridge Companion to Arabic Philosophy* (edited by Peter Adamson and Richard C. Taylor, 2005), for example, emphasizes the period from the ninth to the twelfth centuries, but also includes chapters on Suhrawardī and later Shīʿī Iranian philosophy, and its chapter on logic acknowledges and develops the insights of Rescher concerning thirteenth-century Arabic logic. In recent years, however, the field has moved decisively beyond the points made by Corbin, Nasr, and Rescher in the 1960s, and it is high time for a new presentation that reflects this fact. It is now generally recognized that Corbin and Nasr unduly stressed the Platonist-mystical-Shīʿī synthesis of later centuries. Especially Hossein Ziai and John Walbridge have drawn attention to aspects of the Illuminationist philosophical tradition such as physics and logic that were of little interest to Corbin and Nasr (see especially Ziai 1990; Ziai and Alwishah 2003; Walbridge 2005; Ziai 2010; Walbridge 2012).

At the same time, it is beginning to emerge that there is a largely untold story of continued philosophical activity outside Illuminationist and Shīʿī-Iranian circles. Particularly the work of Dimitri Gutas, A. I. Sabra, Ayman Shihadeh, and Rob Wisnovsky has drawn attention to the fact that the supposed demise of philosophy in the (majority) Sunnī Islamic world is a myth (Gutas 2002; Sabra 1994; Shihadeh 2005; Wisnovsky 2004b, 2013). It may be that the word *falsafa* ("philosophy") was typically avoided due to association with specific ideas deemed heretical by mainstream religious scholars (for example, the eternity of the world, the denial of the possibility of miracles, the denial of God's knowledge of particulars in the sublunary world, and the denial of bodily resurrection). However, a great deal of "philosophy" in the modern sense of the word was still pursued under other names. Especially the field of Islamic theology (*kalām*) became thoroughly suffused in later centuries with terminology, issues, and modes of argumentation derived from Greek philosophy. Widely studied handbooks of theology after the twelfth century typically devoted considerable attention to thoroughly rational discussions of philosophical topics such as the nature of knowledge, the relation between essence and existence, the soul and its relation to the body, the ten Aristotelian categories, predication, modality, the nature of time and space, physics and cosmology (see, for example, the table of contents of one such theological handbook translated in Calverley and Pollock 2002, or the contribution by Alnoor Dhanani to the present volume, on another handbook from the fourteenth century). The study of logic also became incorporated into the curricula of Islamic colleges (madrasas) in later centuries, and the continued vitality of the later tradition of logic even beyond the thirteenth century has been brought out by recent research (for example El-Rouayheb 2010). The upshot is that sophisticated epistemological, metaphysical, natural-philosophical, and logical discussions in later centuries were often carried out by scholars who did not self-identify as *falāsifa* largely because they would have associated the term with acceptance of an Aristotelian and/or Neoplatonic cosmology.

Supplementing these recent insights have been a number of further developments in the field. In the past decades, there has been a steady stream of modern editions of philosophical works, largely thanks to the efforts of modern scholars in the Islamic world. According to the older vision of Corbin and Nasr, Mullā Ṣadrā Shīrāzī (d. 1045/1635) marked the culmination of the later Islamic philosophical tradition. Nevertheless, recent years has seen editions of works by important later philosophers active in Iran, some of whom were highly critical of Mullā Ṣadrā, such as Rajab ʿAlī Tabrīzī (d. 1080/1669), Āqā Ḥusayn Khwānsārī (d. 1098/1687), and Aḥmad Aḥsāʾī (d. 1243/1826) (see, for example, Hiravī and Bayraq 2007; Iṣfahānī 1999; Bū ʿAlī 2007). Furthermore, the older narrative of later Islamic philosophy tended to jump from Suhrawardī in the twelfth century to Mullā Ṣadrā in the seventeenth. Recent editions and studies have drawn attention to important figures in the intervening centuries, such as Ibn Kammūna (d. 683/1284), Quṭb al-Dīn al-Shīrāzī (d. 711/1311), Ibn Abī Jumhūr al-Aḥsāʾī (fl. 883/1479), and Najm al-Dīn Nayrīzī (fl. 928/1522). (See, for example, Walbridge 1992; Schmidtke 2000; Schmidtke and Pourjavady 2006; Ḥabībī 2009; Pourjavady 2011.) There has also been an awakening of interest in Ottoman philosophy in recent years in Turkey, with scholars beginning to edit works by important figures such as Ṭāşköprüzāde (d. 968/1561), Ebū Saʿīd Ḫādimī (d. 1176/1762), and Ismāʿīl Gelenbevī (d. 1205/1790) (see Gül 2009; Konevi and Konevi 2012; Öküdan 2007). Later Indo-Islamic philosophy is also beginning to receive some of the attention it deserves, especially in the work of Asad Q. Ahmed and Sajjad Rizvi (see, for example, Ahmed 2013a, 2013b; Rizvi, 2011).

Equally important, there has lately been a significant re-evaluation of the literary forms of commentary (*sharḥ*) and gloss (*ḥāshiyah*). For much of the twentieth century, the predominant assumption was that the commentaries and glosses of later centuries were pedantic and uncritical expositions that would not merit closer examination. However, this was largely an "armchair" assumption not grounded in a patient examination of these works. In recent years, the older view has been questioned, and more and more scholars are coming to recognize that commentaries and glosses were important vehicles for critical reflection in later centuries (see especially Wisnovsky 2004a; Ahmed 2013b). The fifteenth-century Persian scholar Jalāl al-Dīn al-Dawānī (d. 908/1502), for example, was arguably one of the most innovative and influential of later Islamic philosophers. Yet his major writings—widely studied for centuries in Iran, India, and the Ottoman Empire—took the form of commentaries and glosses on works by earlier figures (see Reza Pourjavady's contribution to this volume for further details).

I.2. A New Presentation of the Field

The present volume is different from earlier overviews in two conspicuous ways. First, as mentioned above, it strives to give roughly equal weight to every century from the ninth to the twentieth. Second, its entries are work centered rather than person or theme centered. In other words, contributors focus, after briefly introducing a philosopher's life and oeuvre, on one major work and give a relatively detailed exposé of it. Article-length entries on individual philosophers can be excellent, but they often have to sacrifice depth to breadth. Entries on movements would have to sacrifice depth to breadth to an even greater degree, and would risk becoming little more than a list of names and titles. Entries on themes are arguably not feasible given the present stage of research. Too few contemporary scholars have a solid command of both earlier and later Islamic philosophical literature, and thematic entries would risk being slanted toward the earlier centuries and more well-known figures at the expense of the later period and lesser-known figures. Particularly at a time when the canon of Islamic philosophy is being reconsidered and new figures and works are emerging from undeserved obscurity, a thematic approach would be counterproductive.

The work-centered format is also intended to allow room for the attention to detail and sustained exposition that are often sacrificed in article-length surveys of the entire range of contributions by an individual philosopher. This should hopefully give the reader a better sense of what a work in Islamic philosophy looks like and a better idea of the issues, concepts, and arguments that are at play in works belonging to various periods and subfields within Islamic philosophy.

The selection of entries has aimed to bring out the uninterrupted history of Islamic philosophy down to the modern period, and to emphasize the fact that philosophical activity in later centuries was not confined to one region of the Islamic world and was not exclusively preoccupied with a single set of issues. Works that were the product of the vibrant philosophical scene in Iran in the Safavid (1501–1722) and Qajar (1779–1925) periods have been supplemented by including less-known works from Egypt, Ottoman Turkey, and Mughal India, and later works with the expected focus on metaphysics and ontology have been supplemented with works on logic and natural philosophy. The twentieth-century works that are covered include an attempt by a traditionally trained Shīʿī scholar to solve Hume's problem of induction, and an influential Egyptian philosopher's adaptation of the ideas of the logical positivists. By covering such works, we hope to challenge a widespread assumption that later Islamic philosophy is necessarily an arcane (or peculiarly "spiritual") discipline that, for better or worse, bears little relation to the concerns of modern Western analytic philosophers.

Though one of the aims of the present work has been to broaden the geographic and temporal scope of the field of Islamic philosophy, some major figures and works that ideally should have been included have unfortunately had to be left out. Inevitably, some of the scholars who were asked to contribute to the volume were unable to do so, for reasons ranging from prior commitments to medical issues. Though we actively sought contributions from scholars who are based in the Islamic world, many of these scholars were not comfortable writing in English. Due to such factors, our volume has had to forgo including contributions on works by, for example, the important logician and philosophical theologian Saʿd al-Dīn al-Taftāzānī (d. 792/1390), the Ottoman scholars Ahmed Ṭāşköprüzāde and Ismāʿīl Gelenbevī, as well as Safavid and post-Safavid philosophers such as Ghiyāth al-Dīn Dashtakī (d. 948/1542), Rajab ʿAlī Tabrīzī, Mahdī Narāqī (d. 1209/1795), and Aḥmad Aḥsāʾī.

There is a long-standing dispute over whether to call the field of study "Arabic philosophy" or "Islamic philosophy." Neither term is entirely satisfactory. The term "Arabic philosophy" is often deemed offensive by non-Arab Muslims. To some extent, this might be because it is difficult to capture the distinction made in English between "Arabic" (a linguistic designation) and "Arab" (an ethnic designation) in some relevant languages. In Arabic and Persian, for example, both would be translated as *ʿarabī*, and the term "Arab philosophy" is clearly both inadequate and offensive. But even the linguistic term "Arabic" elides the fact that especially in later centuries philosophical works were written in Persian and Turkish (and even English, as in the case of Muhammad Iqbal). At the same time, the term "Islamic philosophy" does not do justice to the role of non-Muslims in this tradition, for example the Christians Ḥunayn ibn Isḥāq (d. 260/873), Yaḥyā ibn ʿAdī (d. 363/974), and Abū l-Faraj Ibn al-Ṭayyib (d. 434/1043), or the Zoroastrian student of Avicenna Bahmanyār (d. 457/1065), or the Jewish philosophers Abū l-Barakāt al-Baghdādī (d. 560/1165) and Ibn Kammūna. Furthermore, some contributors to the tradition, such as Abū Bakr al-Rāzī (d. 313/925), were born Muslims but came to reject fundamental precepts of the Islamic religion (such as prophecy). In light of these difficulties, some modern scholars prefer locutions such as "philosophy in the Islamic world" or even "Islamicate philosophy," but the first of these is unwieldy and the second unfamiliar. In the end, there are more important tasks than getting bogged down in issues of nomenclature. "Islamic philosophy" may not be ideal, but a choice had to be made, and it may be less unsatisfactory than the alternatives.

References

Ahmed, Asad Q. 2013a. "Logic in the Khayrābādī School of India: A Preliminary Exploration." In *Law and Tradition in Classical Islamic Thought: Studies in Honor of Professor Hossein Modarressi*, ed. Michael Cook, Najam Haider, Intisar Rabb, and Asma Sayeed. New York: Palgrave, 227–47.

Ahmed, Asad Q. 2013b. "Post-classical Philosophical Commentaries/Glosses: Innovation in the Margins." *Oriens* 41: 317–48.

Bū ʿAlī, Tawfīq Nāṣir. 2007. *Aḥmad al-Aḥsāʾī, Sharḥ al-Mashāʿir*. Beirut: Muʾassasat al-Balāgh.

Calverley, E. E., and J. W. Pollock. 2002. *Nature, Man and God in Medieval Islam: ʿAbd Allah Baydawi's Text, "Tawaliʿ al-anwar min mataliʿ al-anzar", along with Mahmud Isfahani's commentary, "Mataliʿ al-anzar, sharh Tawaliʿ al-anwar"*. Leiden: Brill.

Corbin, Henry. 1945. *Suhrawardi: Opera metaphysica et mystica*. Istanbul: Maarif Matbaasi.

Corbin, Henry. 1964. *Histoire de la philosophie islamique*. Paris: Gallimard.

De Boer, T. J. 1901. *Geschichte der Philosophie im Islam*. Stuttgart: Frommanns Verlag.

El-Rouayheb, Khaled. 2010. *Relational Syllogisms and the History of Arabic Logic, 900–1900*. Leiden: Brill.

Fākhūrī, Ḥanna al-, and Khalīl al-Jurr. 1957. *Tārīkh al-falsafa al-ʿarabiyya*. Beirut: Dār al-Maʿārif.

Gül, Mehmed Zahit Kamil. 2009. *Aḥmed Ṭāşköprüzāde, al-Shuhūd al-ʿaynī fī mabāḥith al-wujūd al-dhihnī*. Cologne: Manshūrāt al-Jamal.

Gutas, Dimitri. 2002. "The Heritage of Avicenna: The Golden Age of Arabic Philosophy, 1000–ca. 1350." In *Avicenna and His Heritage*, ed. J. L. Janssens and D. De Smet. Leuven: Leuven University Press, 81–97.

Ḥabībī, Najafqulī. 2009. *Ibn Kammūna, Sharḥ al-Talwīḥāt al-lawḥiyya wa-al-ʿarshiyya*. Tehran: Markaz al-Buḥūth wa-al-Dirāsāt lil-Turāth al-Makhṭūṭ.

Hiravī, ʿAzīz Javānpūr, and Ḥasan Akbar Bayraq. 2007. *Mullā Rajab ʿAlī Tabrīzī, al-Aṣl al-aṣīl*. Tehran: Mu'assasat-i Muṭālaʿāt-i Islāmī-i Dānishgāh-i Tihrān.

Iṣfahānī, Ḥāmid Nājī. 1999. *Āqā Ḥusayn al-Khwānsārī, al-Ḥāshīyah ʿalā l-Shifā' (al-Ilāhīyāt)*. Qom: Kungrih-i Āqā Ḥusayn Khwānsārī.

Konevi, Hasan, and Mehmet Konevi. 2012. *Ebū Saʿīd Ḫādimī, ʿArā'is al-nafā'is fī al-manṭiq*. Beirut: Dār Ibn Ḥazm.

Madkour, Ibrahim. 1934. *L'Organon d'Aristote dans le monde arabe*. Paris: Vrin.

Nasr, Seyyed Hossein. 1961. "Sadr al-Din Shirazi: His Life, Doctrine and Significance." *Indo-Iranica* 14: 4–16.

Nasr, Seyyed Hossein. 1964. *Three Muslim Sages: Avicenna, Suhrawardi, Ibn ʿArabī*. Cambridge, MA: Harvard University Press.

Öküdan, Mehmet Zühdü. 2007. *Ismāʿīl Gelenbevī, Risāla fī waḥdat al-wujūd*. Isparta: Fakülte Kitabevi.

O'Leary, De Lacy. 1922. *Arabic Thought and Its Place in History*. London: K. Paul, Trench, Trübner; New York: E. P. Dutton.

Pourjavady, Reza. 2011. *Philosophy in Early Safavid Iran: Najm al-Dīn Maḥmūd al-Nayrīzī and His Writings*. Leiden: Brill.

Rescher, Nicholas. 1964. *The Development of Arabic Logic*. Pittsburgh: University of Pittsburgh Press.

Rescher, Nicholas. 1967. *Temporal Modalities in Arabic Logic*. Dordrecht: Reidel.

Rizvi, Sajjad. 2011. "Mīr Dāmād in India: Islamic Philosophical Traditions and the Problem of Creation." *Journal of the American Oriental Society* 131: 9–23.

Sabra, A. I. 1994. "Science and Philosophy in Medieval Islamic Theology: The Evidence of the Fourteenth Century." *Zeitschrift für Geschichte der Arabisch-Islamischen Wissenschaften* 9 (1994): 1–42.

Schmidtke, Sabine. 2000. *Theologie, Philosophie und Mystik im zwölferschiitischen Islam des 9./15. Jahrhunderts: Die Gedankenwelten des Ibn Abī Ǧumhūr al-Aḥsā'ī (um 838/1434–35—nach 905/1501)*. Leiden: Brill.

Schmidtke, Sabine, and Reza Pourjavady. 2006. *A Jewish Philosopher of Baghdad: ʿIzz al-Dawla Ibn Kammuna (d. 683/1284) and His Writings*. Leiden: Brill.

Walbridge, John. 1992. *The Science of Mystic Lights: Quṭb al-Dīn Shīrāzī and the Illuminationist Tradition in Islamic Philosophy*. Cambridge, MA: Center for Middle East Studies.

Walbridge, John. 2005. "Al-Suhrawardī on Body as Extension: An Alternative to Hylomorphism from Plato to Leibniz." In *Reason and Inspiration in Islam: Theology,*

Philosophy and Mysticism in Muslim Thought. Essays in Honour of Hermann Landolt, ed. Todd Lawson. London: I.B. Tauris, 235–47.

Walbridge, John. 2012. "Illuminationists, Place, and the Void." In *La nature et le vide dans la physique medieval*, ed. Joël Biard and Sabine Rommevaux. Turnhout: Brepols, 119–36.

Watt, W. Montgomery. 1962. *Islamic Philosophy and Theology*. Edinburgh: Edinburgh University Press.

Wisnovsky, Rob. 2004a. "The Nature and Scope of Arabic Philosophical Commentary in Post-Classical (ca. 1100–1900 AD) Islamic Intellectual History." In *Philosophy, Science and Exegesis in Greek, Arabic and Latin Commentaries*, ed. P. Adamson, H. Balthussen, and M. W. F. Stone. London: Institute of Advanced Studies, 2:149–91.

Wisnovsky, Rob. 2004b. "One Aspect of the Avicennian Turn in Sunnī Theology." *Arabic Sciences and Philosophy* 14: 65–100.

Wisnovsky, Rob. 2013. "Avicenna's Islamic Reception." In *Interpreting Avicenna: Critical Essays*, ed. Peter Adamson. Cambridge: Cambridge University Press, 190–213.

Ziai, Hossein. 1990. *Knowledge and Illumination: A Study of Suhrawardī's Ḥikmat al-ishrāq*. Atlanta: Scholar's Press.

Ziai, Hossein. 2010. *Ṣadr al-Dīn Shīrāzī: Addenda on the Commentary on the Philosophy of Illumination, Pt. 1: On the Rules of Thought*. Costa Mesa, CA: Mazda Publishers.

Ziai, Hossein, and A. Alwishah. 2003. *Ibn Kammūna: al-Tanqīḥāt fī sharḥ al-Talwīḥāt: Refinement and Commentary on Suhrawardī's Intimations, a Thirteenth Century Text on Natural Philosophy and Psychology*. Costa Mesa, CA: Mazda Publishers.

CHAPTER 1

THE *THEOLOGY* ATTRIBUTED TO ARISTOTLE

Sources, Structure, Influence

CRISTINA D'ANCONA

1.1. The Pseudo-*Theology of Aristotle*: Some Facts

The first explicit quotation from a work named *Theology* by the pen of "Aristotle" features in al-Fārābī's *Harmonization of the Two Opinions of the Two Sages, Plato the Divine and Aristotle* (Martini Bonadeo 2008, 74:5–16 in Arabic; Butterworth 2001, 164–65 in English),[1] and the *Theology* is listed among Aristotle's works in the *Kitāb al-Fihrist* by Ibn al-Nadīm (ed. Flügel 252.4 = ed. Tajaddud, 312.20). If we take into account the title of a collection allegedly translated by Abū ʿUthmān al-Dimashqī (fl. 302/914)[2] of texts that

[1] Critical edition by Martini Bonadeo (2008), English trans. by Butterworth (2001). The Farabian authorship of this text has been challenged (see the dossier in Martini Bonadeo 2008, 28–30). Endress (2008) and Martini Bonadeo (2008) hold the text to be authentic; Rashed (2009) and Gleede (2012) maintain that it is spurious. The question of the authorship of this work does not affect the issue of the mention of "Aristotle's" *Theology* in it. As far as we know, the *Harmonization* is the first work in which the *Theology* is ascribed to "Aristotle"; given that none of the scholars who challenge the Farabian authorship of this writing advances a candidate either earlier or much later than al-Fārābī (d. 339/950), this elicits the conclusion that toward the middle of the tenth century the *Theology* was known as a work by Aristotle. Besides the literal quotation from Aristotle's *Theology*, mention of the text occurs in various places: 64.7; 64.15–65.14; 69.15–70.7 Martini Bonadeo, English trans. by Butterworth (2001), 155–57, 161.

[2] The *floruit* of Abū ʿUthmān al-Dimashqī is given by the year of his appointment as the director of the hospital founded by the vizier ʿAlī b. ʿĪsā (d. 334/946). One of the most prominent scholars of his age, Abū ʿUthmān al-Dimashqī was a pupil of Isḥāq b. Ḥunayn (d. 289/910), and the author of many translations of scientific and philosophical works: see the entry by G. Endress in *Encyclopedia of Islam*, 8: 858. The alleged "extracts by Alexander" from the "*Theology* by Aristotle" are in fact some *Questions* by Alexander of Aphrodisias and some propositions of Proclus's *Elements of Theology*, as shown by van Ess (1966) and

"Alexander extracted from Aristotle's *Theology*" (Rosenthal 1955; van Ess 1966; Endress 1973, 34), the conclusion imposes itself that in the fourth/tenth century the exposure of the cultivated Arab readership to Neoplatonism in Aristotle's garb was an accomplished fact. That the *Theology* quoted in the *Harmonization* is nothing if not the adapted Arabic version of Plotinus is made evident by a passage as literal as to feature in the discussion of the textual tradition of the pseudo-*Theology* itself (Zimmermann 1986, 140). That the *Theology* alluded to in the *Harmonization* did also contain other Neoplatonic texts, namely parts of the Arabic version of Proclus's *Elements of Theology*, has been convincingly argued (Endress 1973, 246; Zimmermann 1986, 178–80). All this suggests that in the philosophical circles of that age various texts were available, gathered under the common reference to Aristotle as their author, but issued in reality from Neoplatonic literature: among them, the well-known *Book of the Exposition by Aristotle on the Pure Good* (*Liber de Causis*), which was known as a work by "Aristotle" by the end of the fourth/tenth century (Rowson 1984). The most important of these pseudepigrapha is the *Theology* par excellence: the adapted translation of selected writings from the *Enneads*. The *Theology of Aristotle* was the main conduit through which Plotinus's doctrines were known in the Arabic-speaking world, a fact that has been aptly described as the "power of anonymity" that Plotinus held on Arabic philosophical literature (Rosenthal 1974).

If the mid-fourth/tenth century openly credits Aristotle with a Neoplatonic *Theology*, this does not imply that the latter remained unknown to or scarcely influential on earlier writers. The contrary is true: the Arabic adapted version of Plotinus (henceforth ps.-*Theology*) is echoed in several works from the second half of the third/ninth century onward. But before we turn to the doctrines of the ps.-*Theology* and to their influence, it may be well to recall the main data about the text itself.

The ps.-*Theology* has come down to us in two versions: one in Arabic, transmitted by more than one hundred manuscripts,[3] and another one that is fully extant in Latin and is fragmentarily attested in Judeo-Arabic (Borisov [1942] 2002; Fenton 1986; Aouad 1989, 564–70; Treiger 2007). The Latin version is transmitted by the editio princeps

Endress (1973, 33–40). Some by Alexander, and all the texts of Proclus in this collection, trace back to a stage of the translations into Arabic that is earlier than Dimashqī's, as has been proved by Endress (1973, 59, 75–76). The reason why al-Dimashqī is mentioned as the translator lies in that he probably translated part of Alexander's *Questions* present in this collection, gathering also earlier materials. This elicits the conclusion that these earlier materials included not only Plotinus, but also Proclus and some Alexander. For the present purposes, the relevant point is that the learned audience of Dimashqī's times knew of the *Theology* by "Aristotle" that was in fact based on post-Aristotelian materials, most of them Neoplatonic (see Zimmermann 1986, 185).

[3] The two editions of this version of the ps.-*Theology* (see below, note 5) are based on very few and random manuscripts. The study of the manuscript tradition of the ps.-*Theology* has been substantially improved, first in the 1950s, thanks to the research surrounding the critical edition of the *Enneads*, and then by G. Endress, who has established an unpublished list of more than forty manuscripts. The critical edition of the ps.-*Theology* is currently being prepared by a research team of the ERC AdG 249431 "Greek into Arabic: Philosophical Concepts and Linguistic Bridges." The list established by Prof. Endress counted as the starting point for the teamwork. Thanks to the support of the European Research Council, the team has raised the number of the known manuscripts of the ps.-*Theology* to more than one hundred.

published in Rome in 1519 (Mariën 1973, 608–10) and bears the title *Aristotle's Theology, this is to say the mystical philosophy according to the Egyptians.*[4] This text differs from the Arabic one on various counts. To mention only the blatant differences, it falls into fourteen chapters instead of the ten of the Arabic text, and the so-called Headings of the Questions (see below, section 1.2) do not feature in it; should one go deeper into the comparison, a mismatch would appear here and there, both in wording and in structure. Partly different from the Arabic, the Latin proves to be akin to the fragments in Judeo-Arabic, so paving the way to the conclusion (Borisov [1942] 2002) that the Latin translation was made on the basis of a full text, lost to us, of which only the Judeo-Arabic fragments survive, and which was somehow different from the Arabic text. Indeed, both in these fragments and in the Latin version some passages feature that are lacking in the Arabic text; hence, the work that lies in the background of the Latin has been labeled "Long Version." It has been convincingly argued (Pines 1954) that the "Long Version" included materials of Ismāʿīlī provenance added to the original (Stern 1960–61; Fenton 1986, 245–51), that is, to the text that we can read in Arabic and that is at times labeled "the *vulgata*"—a label that reflects more the poor quality of its editions to date[5] than the real nature of this work. The present chapter deals with the so-called *vulgata*, namely the Arabic ps.-*Theology*.

The title runs: "The first chapter of the book of Aristotle the Philosopher, called in Greek Theologia (*Uthūlūjiyā*), being the discourse on Divine Sovereignty: Porphyry the Syrian interpreted it, and it was translated into Arabic by ʿAbd al-Masīḥ b. Nāʿima of Emessa and was corrected for Aḥmad b. al-Muʿtaṣim bi-llāh by Abū Yūsuf Yaʿqūb b. Isḥāq al-Kindī" (ed. Badawī 3.3–9; trans. Lewis 1959, 486, slightly modified). This title provides both a terminus ante quem for the translation of (parts of) the *Enneads* into Arabic, and valuable information about the milieu in which the ps.-*Theology* was created. The terminus ante quem for the translation, made by the Christian Ibn Nāʿima al-Ḥimsī,[6] is the reign of the caliph al-Muʿtaṣim (r. 218/833–227/842), whose son Aḥmad had al-Kindī as

[4] The full title runs *Sapientissimi philosophi Aristotelis Stagiritae Theologia sive mystica philosophia secundum Aegyptios noviter reperta et in latinum castigatissime redacta.* The allusion to the Egyptians points to a passage in which Plotinus mentions the wise men of Egypt (V 8[31], 6.1 = ps.-*Theology*, ed. Badawī 1955, 10, 159.16). In the fiction of the *Theology*, this turns to be an utterance by Aristotle himself. As we are told in the preface to the Latin version, this helps to explain why the doctrines of the *Theology* are so different from Aristotle's own ideas: "As a matter of fact, Aristotle says here—something he does nowhere else—that he is accounting not for his own lore, but for other's, the Egyptians" (*etenim Aristotelis hic aperte praefatur, quod nusquam alibi, se non propriam, sed alienam Aegyptiorum sapientiam colligere*: Proemium, A [4v26–29]).

[5] *Editio princeps*: Dieterici (1882); *editio manualis*: Badawī (1955, repr. 1966). The poor quality of the *editio princeps* is occasionally remarked by Rosenthal (1952–55, 466); on the poor quality of the *editio manualis* see Lewis 1957.

[6] This name is repeated also at the beginning of the so-called Headings of the Questions (see below), where it is spelled ʿAbd al-Masīḥ al-Ḥimṣī al-Nāʿimī (8.4 Badawī). The full name as it is given in the *K. al-Fihrist* is ʿAbd al-Masīḥ ibn ʿAbd Allāh al-Ḥimṣī al-Nāʿimī (ed. Flügel, 244.5 = ed. Tajaddud, 304.26), but he is referred to as Ibn Nāʿima in the two entries where he is mentioned, namely that on the *Soph. El.* and that on the *Physics*. He is said (ed. Flügel, 249.27–28 = ed. Tajaddud, 309.9–10) to have translated into

his preceptor. We are told by the title that Aḥmad was the addressee of the adaptation of the work by "Aristotle" called in Greek *Uthūlūjiyā*. We are also told that the corrector was Abū Yūsuf Yaʿqūb b. Isḥāq al-Kindī (d. *c*. 252/866), the "philosopher of the Arabs." This ties in with the view, suggested by several clues, of al-Kindī as engaged in the philosophical education of at least part of the ʿAbbāsid court (Rosenthal 1942; Endress 1997 and 2012; Adamson 2007). We owe to Gerhard Endress not only the discovery of the common style of a set of translations from Greek into Arabic originated within the "circle of al-Kindī" (Endress 1997), but also the key to understanding why he engaged so strenuously in the assimilation of Greek metaphysics. Endress has highlighted that al-Kindī's "programme *de propaganda philosophia*, which came into being as an ideology of scientists heirs to the Hellenistic encyclopaedia and as a religion for intellectuals compatible with Islam, was a programme for the integration of philosophy and the rational sciences into Muslim Arab society" (Endress 2000, 569; see also Endress 2007). Against this backdrop, it comes as no surprise that Plotinus's doctrines are construed as the exposition genuinely made by Aristotle himself of the pinnacle of the *Metaphysics*, a work whose translation into Arabic was commissioned by al-Kindī (*al-Fihrist*, ed. Flügel, 251.27–28 = ed. Tajaddud, 312.14). The *Metaphysics* is echoed at the very beginning of the ps.-*Theology* and counts as the main source of inspiration for al-Kindī's own work *On the First Philosophy* (Abū Rīda 1950; Rashed and Jolivet 1999; English trans. Ivry 1974).

The ps.-*Theology* opens with the claim that whoever wants to reach the knowledge of the ultimate end (*al-ghāya*) must seek for absolute certainty and conform in his behavior to the ideal of the ascent in the scientific disciplines toward contemplative life (ed. Badawī, 3.10–4.2). Then the writer gives the floor to the Sage, whose words are announced by the formula "the Sage said" (*qāla l-ḥakīm*, ed. Badawī, 4.3). The discourse of the Sage points to the final cause as the goal that, although coming last, sets the tone for all that has been done before: this theory of an Aristotelian flavor is expressed by the saying "first desired last attained" (Stern 1962; see also Zimmermann 1986, 111). The goal is described as the knowledge of the ultimate truth in theoretical sciences, and the path toward it is presented as a collective achievement of the leading philosophers (*afāḍil al-falāsifa*, ed. Badawī, 4.10). They all agree on the fact that the first causes of the universe are four: matter, form, the efficient cause, and perfection (ed. Badawī, 4.11). The Sage continues his account by saying that he has devoted to this topic a book named *baʿd al-ṭabīʿiyyāt*, "what is after the physical realities" (ed. Badawī, 4.11–5.2), a claim that leaves no room to doubt that the Sage speaking is "Aristotle." An overview of the *Metaphysics* follows, whose pivot is the topic of wisdom as the knowledge of causes, clearly reminiscent of the first book of the *Metaphysics*. Also the allusion to the philosophers of the past as engaged in the etiological inquiry traces back to the beginning of the

Syriac the *Soph. El.* He also translated part of Aristotle's *Physics* with the commentary by Philoponus (ed. Flügel, 250.18 = ed. Tajaddud, 311.1). Ibn Nāʿima is mentioned also in the Latin version, not in the title (where only Aristotle appears: see above) but in the preface by Pietro Castellani, the "editor" of the Latin version (*Theologia Aristotelis a graeca lingua pridem per Abenamam saracenum in arabam translatum*, Proemium, A [4r8–10]).

Metaphysics. This account ends with another mention of this work, now called "Book of the Metaphysics," *Kitāb Maṭāṭāfūsīqā*" (ed. Badawī, 5.12). According to the Sage, the book of the *Metaphysics* contains the premises (*muqaddimāt*, ed. Badawī, 5.10) of the discourse on the Divine Sovereignty that is about to begin (ed. Badawī, 6.7), a label echoed in the title mentioned above: "Theologia (*Uthūlūjiyā*), being the discourse on Divine Sovereignty (*qawl ʿalā l-rubūbiyya*)."

As we have seen before, the contents of this "discourse on Divine Sovereignty" are extracted from a selection of the *Enneads*, that is, the systematic edition of Plotinus's writings provided by Porphyry. In his *Life of Plotinus and Order of His Books* published together with the *Enneads*, Porphyry says he had been inspired in his arrangement by Andronicus's thematic ordering of the *corpus Aristotelicum* (Porph. *Vita Plotini*, 24.5–11). The first three groups of nine treatises ("enneads") were devoted to man and the cosmos; the fourth ennead to soul; the fifth to the intelligible world; the sixth and last to the One, the first principle of Plotinus's universe. Of all this, only a part is attested in Arabic. The treatises translated come all from *Enneads* IV–VI, a fact that tips the scale in favor of a deliberate selection of topics, ruling out the hypothesis of a defective Greek model of the Arabic version. Even though there is no attestation of the treatises of *Enneads* I–III in Arabic, the manuscript of the *Enneads* out of which the translation was made must have been complete of the beginning; otherwise it would have been impossible to connect with the *Enneads* the name of Porphyry, which features in the title of the ps.-*Theology*. In fact, Porphyry's *Vita Plotini* does not have an independent circulation, but is premised to the *Enneads*; since in the ps.-*Theology* Porphyry is mentioned, it is fair to assume that the Greek manuscript, which was at the disposal of the translator, contained also the *Vita Plotini* and, by extension, the *Enneads* from their beginning. Be this as it may, what was considered worthy of being translated was the part dealing with the suprasensible principles: *Enneads* IV, V, and VI.

Plotinus's One, Intellect, and Soul feature in the following statement by "Aristotle" as the natural complement of the doctrines expounded in the *Metaphysics*:

> Now since we have completed the customary prefaces, which are principles that lead on to the explanation of what we wish to explain in this book of ours, let us not waste words over this branch of knowledge, since we have already given an account of it in the book of the Metaphysics . . . . Now our aim in this book is the discourse on the Divine Sovereignty, and the explanation of it, and how it is the first cause, eternity and time being beneath it, and that it is the cause and the originator of causes, in a certain way, and how the luminous force steals from it over Mind and, through the medium of Mind, over the universal celestial Soul, and from Mind, through the medium of Soul, over nature, and from Soul, through the medium of nature, over the things that come to be and pass away. This action arises from it without motion: the motion of all things comes from it and is caused by it, and things move towards it by a kind of longing and desire. (ps.-*Theol. Arist.*, ed. Badawī, 5.10–6.12; trans. Lewis 1959, 487)

It is apparent from this statement that Plotinus's One and Aristotle's Unmoved Mover merge together, and that the Plotinian principles Intellect and Soul are endowed with the task to let the power of the First Cause expand until it reaches the world of coming-to-be and passing away. Two accounts of the way in which the First Cause acts are combined: the Plotinian emanation from the One and the Aristotelian capability of the Unmoved Mover to impart movement as the object of desire (ὡς ἐρώμενον, *Metaph.* Λ.7, 1072b3). It comes as no surprise that the Aristotelian authorship of the ps.-*Theology* remained unchallenged for centuries, leading the most percipient readers of the past (who noticed that the *Theology* gives, despite everything, a distinct non-Aristotelian ring) to speculate about the causes of this discrepancy. One of the most ingenious attempts at accounting for the discrepancy has been made by Francesco Patrizi da Cherso in his 1591 work *Nova de universis philosophia*, to which the Latin version of the ps.-*Theology* is appended. According to Patrizi, Aristotle in his old age went back to the doctrines he had heard in his youth from Plato's own mouth: the "unwritten doctrines" whose similarity with Neoplatonic metaphysics has been remarked time and again, and to which Patrizi refers. That the doctrines held in the *Theology* were of "Platonic" coin was remarked in early modern times by Johannes Fabricius in the *Bibliotheca Graeca* (Fabricius 1716, 162),[7] and the name of Plotinus was connected with the ps.-*Theology* first in Thomas Taylor's harsh account of this text as a forgery (Taylor 1812, III, 402), then in Salomon Munk's *Mélanges de philosophie juive et arabe* (Munk 1859, 248), and again in the review by Valentin Rose of the German translation of the ps.-*Theology* (Rose 1883) that inaugurated modern research on the Arabic Plotinus.

Yet close as the ps.-*Theology* is to Plotinus, there are also many differences between the Arabic version and the original text. First and foremost, the flow of the Greek has been substantially altered, and blocks of Plotinus's treatises are relocated, in what seems to be complete disorder. Second, misunderstandings, adaptations, and changes of meaning surface everywhere, and long passages feature in the ps.-*Theology*, that have no counterpart in the *Enneads*. Both the differences and the interpolations have been accounted for in past scholarship by advancing the hypothesis that the Arabic text was the translation not of the Greek *Enneads* but of another work, in which Plotinus's wording and thought had already undergone adaptations of various kinds. Among them are omnipresent the monotheistic adaptations that transform the One into God the Almighty and its causality into creation out of nothing. Given that some words of Syriac origin[8] or allegedly

[7] The quote reads: "This work deals with God, *Logos*, soul, the cosmos, and the principles of things, not in Aristotelian vein, but more or less in the way of the Hermetic *Poemandres*, so that the very nature of this work makes it clear that its author is a Platonist, rather than Aristotle" (*In hoc opere de Deo,* λόγῳ, *anima, universo rerumque principiis non aristotelico more, sed ita fere ut in hermetico Poemandro sic disseritur, ut platonicum potius aliquem quam Aristotelem auctorem esse res ipsa clamet*).

[8] As is the case with *mīmar* for "chapter," a fact that from Baumstark (1902) onward has been adduced as evidence of the Syriac origin of the text. In the hypothesis of forgery, this is open to another explanation, which ties in with the fact that in the title Porphyry is mentioned as the *Syrian* commentator of the work at hand (*fassarahu Furfūriyyūs al-Ṣūrī*, ed. Badawī, 3.6, modified). Porphyry, the writer who gives the floor to "Aristotle" (cf. *qāla l-ḥakīm*, ed. Badawī, 4.3), is presented in this hypothesis as the author of the organization of the materials into chapters (*mayāmir*). For another intervention that in this hypothesis should be ascribed to Porphyry in his capacity of the commentator of Aristotle's *Theology*, see below, section 1.2.

pointing to a Syriac antecedent peer out, the monotheistic adaptations were explained by the hypothesis that an adapted text based on Plotinus had been produced within a Christian milieu in Syria, and that it was such a text, lost to us, that lay in the background of the Arabic version (Baumstark 1902). However, the fact that the ps.-*Theology* is based on the Greek *Enneads* exactly as Porphyry had edited them has been proved beyond any doubt (Schwyzer 1941). In addition, there is no hard evidence pointing to a literary item in Syriac that may support the existence of an intermediary text, a fact that led Sebastian Brock to label "a Chimera" the alleged Syriac model of the ps.-*Theology* (Brock 2007).

If the ps.-*Theology* has the Greek *Enneads* as its immediate antecedent, how to explain the differences between the two works? Scholars answer this question by taking into account two other texts, distinct from the ps.-*Theology* but connected to it both because they share in the same adaptations and because one of them overlaps here and there with the ps.-*Theology*. They are the so-called *Sayings of the Greek Sage* (Rosenthal 1952–55, Wakelnig 2014), which at times overlap with the ps.-*Theology* but also contain passages from the Arabic Plotinus lacking in it, and an *Epistle on the Divine Science* falsely attributed to al-Fārābī (Kraus 1940–41), which does not overlap with the ps.-*Theology*, but has one passage in common with the *Sayings*. These two texts prove the existence of an "Arabic Plotinus Source" (Rosenthal 1952–55) wider than the ps.-*Theology* itself. To the same "Arabic Plotinus Source" trace back also other quotations of Plotinus's passages that share in the same adaptations: they have been recently discovered in the early Arabic translation of Aristotle's *Parva naturalia* produced within the "circle of al-Kindī" (Hansberger 2011). All this points to the existence of an adapted Arabic translation of *Enneads* IV–VI, whose terminus ante quem is the ps.-*Theology* created, if we trust its title, in the 220s/840s at the caliphal court of Baghdad.

The creation of the ps.-*Theology* as a work designed by "Aristotle" to fulfill the demand for an exposition of "Divine Sovereignty" has been accounted for in different ways: either as an awkward, later reconstruction of a collection of post-Aristotelian works that had originally been gathered within the "circle of al-Kindī" and was accidentally dismembered (Zimmermann 1986), or as the first attempt, made by al-Kindī himself, to put together a theological pinnacle for the Aristotelian corpus—an attempt not very successful in itself, but paving the way to a most refined outcome, the *Liber de Causis* (D'Ancona 2011). Both explanations are intended to account, although in different ways, for the fact that the chapters of the ps.-*Theology* do not follow the program described at the beginning of this work. This program is presented by "Aristotle" as an outline of what will be dealt with in the *Theology* (ed. Badawī, 6.3–4). He announces that, after having outlined what divine sovereignty is, he will proceed to describe the intelligible world, then the cosmic Soul, then again sublunar nature, and that he will eventually account for the destiny of the individual souls, explaining the cause of their descent in and ascent from the world of coming-to-be and passing away (ed. Badawī, 6.13–7.10). However, the ps.-*Theology* begins not by giving an account of the First Cause, but by raising the problem of the descent of the soul into the body; the other points mentioned by "Aristotle" are extensively dealt with in it, but a clear order cannot be detected in the flow of the chapters.

1.2. A Neoplatonic Model for God's Causality and the Soul's "Provenance and Destination": The Main Topics of the Pseudo-*Theology of Aristotle* and Their Impact on Arabic-Islamic Philosophy

As we have just seen, the main topics that "Aristotle" sets for himself to discuss are divine causality, the hierarchy of the suprasensible principles, and the destiny of the soul. Before dealing extensively with these points, "Aristotle" announces he will list the "Headings of the Questions"—a puzzling item into which we are not compelled to enter here: suffice it to mention that they are 142 short numbered sentences closely connected with chapters 1–34 of *Enn.* IV 4[28], in itself a part of Plotinus's text that is present in the ps.-*Theology* (D'Ancona 2012). After this list, another section of the long first chapter comes:

> To proceed: Now that it has been demonstrated and confirmed that the soul is not a body and does not die or decay or perish, but is abiding and everlasting, we wish to study concerning her also *how she departs from the world of mind and* descends in this corporeal world of sense and *enters this* gross transient *body* which falls under genesis and corruption. (ps.-*Theol. Ar.*, I, ed. Badawī, 18.11–16; trans. Lewis 1959, 219)

Conforming to Lewis's practice, the italics mark the words and sentences taken from Plotinus, and normal typescript indicates those that feature only in the Arabic text. Here, Plotinus's sentence "How then, since the intelligible is separate, does soul come into body?" (IV 7[2], 13.1–2, trans. Armstrong 1984) is encapsulated between two passages that do not come from the *Enneads*, namely a summary of a demonstration allegedly provided elsewhere of the incorporeal and immortal nature of the soul, and the amplification of the term "body" through the Aristotelian pair of generation-corruption, a move that lays emphasis on the corruptible nature of the body in which the soul is dwelling. Although incorporeal and immortal in itself, the soul is united with a body that comes to be and passes away. This raises a problem: if the soul existed prior to the body and its nature is higher than the body's, why on earth should it undergo, or even decide, the embodiment? This problem sets the scene for the rest of the chapter. "Aristotle" had alluded to this question just before announcing his wish to begin by a list of "Headings of the Questions": he had in fact claimed he would have dealt with "the state of the reasoning souls in their descent and their ascent and the discovery of the cause in that" (ed. Badawī, 7.7–8; trans. Lewis 1959, 487).

This problem is obviously a Platonic one: meaningless in the Aristotelian account of the soul, it arises for a Platonist who, sticking to the doctrine of the soul's incorporeality and immortality, has to face the rival notions of soul as the entelechy of the body and as one of its emergent properties. Plotinus was indeed such a Platonist, and in the treatise that is the source of the passage quoted above, namely IV 7[2], *On the Immortality of the Soul*, he spent much effort in arguing against Stoic emergentism and Aristotelian immanentism. After having criticized the rival theories, he presented the real nature of the soul: a substance on its own, independent of and superior to body. Then, in a sort of appendix to the main topic of the treatise, he raised the question that, in the ps.-*Theology*, turns to be the first step of the detailed treatment promised by "Aristotle": if soul is an incorporeal and immortal substance, why on earth does it come into a body? This question, raised in the final part of treatise IV 7[2], *On the Immortality of the Soul*, was so important in Plotinus's eyes that he went back to it in a treatise written shortly after, IV 8[6], *On the Descent of the Soul into the Bodies*. The numbers in square brackets are those of the chronological order in which Plotinus's treatises were written; the other numbers indicate the position assigned to them by Porphyry in the systematic layout—the *Enneads*. The sequence IV 7–IV 8 shows that Porphyry did not fail to notice how close are the conclusion of *On the Immortality of the Soul* and the main topic of *On the Descent of the Soul into the Bodies*: hence, he edited them as the seventh and eighth treatises of the fourth ennead, devoted to the soul. This link did not escape the creator of the ps.-*Theology* either: the first chapter, after "Aristotle's" introduction and the "Headings of the Questions," consists of the final part of the *Immortality of the Soul* and the beginning of the *Descent of the Soul into the Bodies*, linked together in a new literary item whose focus is the cause of the soul's departure from the intelligible world (table 1.1).

Not only does this add further evidence to the dependence of the ps.-*Theology* upon Porphyry's edition: it also indicates that the chapters of the "book by Aristotle the philosopher called in Greek Theology," as imperfect as their flow may be, result from an attempt at creating a new arrangement of the materials taken from Plotinus, a fact that rules out the hypothesis of an inept gathering of leaves accidentally scattered.

In the Greek original, the *Descent of the Soul into the Bodies* begins by a first-person account: "Often I have woken up out of the body to myself and have entered into myself, going out from all other things; I have seen a beauty wonderfully great and felt assurance that then most of all I belonged to the better part; I have actually lived the best life and come to identity with the divine; and set firm in it I have come to that supreme actuality, setting myself above all else in the realm of Intellect" (IV 8[6], 1.1–8, trans. Armstrong 1984). In chapter 1 of the ps.-*Theology*, the connection between the end of the part taken from the *Immortality of the Soul* and the beginning of the first-person account taken from the *Descent of the Soul into the Bodies* is marked by another intervention of the writer who, earlier in the chapter, had given the floor to "Aristotle" by the formula *qāla l-ḥakīm*. This time, the writer accounts for the use of the first person, saying: "A statement of his (*kalām lahu*) that is like an allegory (*ramz*) of the universal soul" (ed. Badawī, 22.1; trans. Lewis 1959, 225). There is no scholarly consensus about the identity of the "Allegorist,"[9] but his *kalām* has been unanimously acknowledged as

[9] The "Allegorist" is referred to also in another passage of the ps.-*Theology*, whose wording points unmistakably to the sentence quoted above. Here is the passage: "*We say that he who is capable of* doffing

Table 1.1 The Greek and Arabic Plotinus

Ennead IV (On Soul)					
Treatise 7 *On the Immortality of the Soul*			Treatise 8 *On the Descent of the Soul into the Bodies*		
1–8 The rival theories	9–12 The true doctrine of soul: a separate, immortal substance	13–15 Appendix: the problem of the descent of the soul into the bodies	1–2 The descent of the soul into the bodies: Plato's account	3–5 The body-soul relationship	6–8 Solution of the problem of the descent: the hierarchy of the levels of being. Appendix: the undescended soul

Ps.-*Theology of Aristotle*, Chapter 1			
Aristotle's introduction to his "Theology," ed. Badawī, 3.1–7.10	Headings of the Questions, ed. Badawī, 8.1–18.10	The reasons of the descent of the soul into the bodies, ed. Badawī, 18.13–21.17 (= IV 7, 13–15 + IV 8, 1–2)	Aristotle's exegesis of Plato's theological doctrine, ed. Badawī, 22.1–28.3

something important for the entire story of Arabic philosophy, and beyond. This passage has been often quoted or alluded to, in Arabic and Jewish philosophy and mysticism: by al-Kindī (*Discourse on the Soul Abridged from the Book of Aristotle, Plato and the Other Philosophers*, ed. Abū Rīda, 277.15–278.2 and 279.10–13), by al-Fārābī (see note 1), in the Epistles of the Ikhwān al-Ṣafā' (ed. Ghālib 1984, I, 138), by Ibn Zurʿa (quoted by al-Bayhaqī, 77.22–78.11, al-ʿAjam 1994), by Abū Yaʿqūb al-Sijistānī (De Smet 2012, 136), and by Ibn Ṭufayl (ed. Gauthier 1981, 120.6–121.3). Other quotations or allusions feature in the works of Moses ibn Ezra, Shemtob ibn Falaqēra, Solomon ibn Gabirol, in the Sufi tradition, and in Jewish mysticism (Altmann 1963).

> *Often I have been* alone *with my soul and have doffed my body and laid it aside* and become as if I were naked substance without body, *so as to be inside myself, outside*

his body and putting to rest its senses and promptings and motions, as the Allegorist (*ṣāḥib al-rumūz*) has described of his own soul, and is capable too in his thought of returning to himself and *raising his mind to the world of mind*, so as to see its beauty and splendour, *is able to recognize the glory, light and splendour of the mind*" (ed. Badawī, 56.4–7; trans. Lewis 1959, 375; the Plotinian passage echoed here is V 8[31], 1.1–2). According to Zimmermann (1986, 145–47), the expression *kalām lahu* (ed. Badawī, 22.1) alludes to Plato; according to D'Ancona et al. (2003, 280–82), to Aristotle. The topic of the allegory, *ramz*, is echoed also in the *Nabatean Agriculture*, a third–fourth-/ninth–tenth-century compilation of late-antique sources that includes also materials coming from the Arabic Plotinus: see Hämeen-Anttila 2006, 30 and 104–8. On the Plotinian passages in the *Nabatean Agriculture* see also Salinger 1971 and Mattila 2007.

> *all other things* and to be knowledge, knower, and known at once.[10] *Then do I see* within myself *such beauty and splendour as I do remain marvelling at and astonished, so that I know that I am one of the parts of the sublime, surpassing, lofty, divine world, and possess active life.* When I am certain of that, *I lift my intellect from that world into the divine cause and become as if I were placed in it and cleaving to it, so as to be above the entire intelligible world, and seem to be standing in that sublime and divine place.* And there I see such light and splendour as tongues cannot describe nor ears comprehend. (ps.-*Theol. Ar.*, ed. Badawī, I, 22.2–9; trans. Lewis 1959, 225, slightly modified)

Following in the footsteps of Plotinus's narrative, the "Allegorist" experiences not only the return of his soul to itself, but also the spiritual union with the intelligible realm,[11] thus paving the way for the creation of one of the most pervasive topics of Arabic philosophy as a whole: that of the conjunction of man's mind with the separate Intellect. The fully fledged version of the theory of the conjunction of man's mind with the separate Intellect will be elaborated only after the translation by Isḥāq b. Ḥunayn of Alexander of Aphrodisias's short writing *On Intellect*, but the latter will be interpreted, both in the Arabic translation and by the philosophers who rely on it, in the light of the ps.-*Theology* (Geoffroy 2002). The influence of the ps.-*Theology* has been detected also on Avicenna's interpretation of the same topic (D'Ancona 2008).

After having experienced this conjunction, the "Allegorist" descends once again in the realm of discursive reasoning. As Plotinus did, he wonders how is it possible that his soul, in spite of the conjunction it had with the divine, descends into a corruptible body and becomes a part of the lower world ruled by coming-to-be and passing away (ed. Badawī, 22.9–15). The answer, as was the case with Plotinus, is provided by the Greek philosophers. The ancient thinkers quoted by Plotinus (Heraclitus, Empedocles, Pythagoras: IV 8[6], 1.11–23) count also for the "Allegorist" as the authoritative voices from the past—a case in point for the "agreement of the leading philosophers" emphasized by "Aristotle" at the beginning. Still following in Plotinus's footsteps (IV 8[6], 1.23–27), he turns now

[10] The words "and to be knowledge, knower, and known at once" do not feature in Lewis's translation because they are lacking in one of the manuscripts of the ps.-*Theology* that is particularly authoritative. The issue cannot be discussed here, but let me mention the fact that these words feature in Fārābī's quotation (see Martini Bonadeo 2008, 74.8). This independent witness, much earlier than the earliest manuscript of the ps.-*Theology* known to us, tips the scale in favor of the branch of the textual tradition that has this sentence.

[11] Plotinus described the individual soul as capable of performing the same cognitive activity as the separate Intellect, and this is different from saying, in the footsteps of St. Paul (1 Cor. 2:9), that one has experienced the direct vision of God. On the Pauline inspiration of the words "And there I see such light and splendour as tongues cannot describe nor ears comprehend," which became also a Prophetic hadith, see Zimmermann 1986, 141–43; see also Bucur and Bucur 2006. Lack of space forbids the treatment of this topic, but let me briefly recall that for Plotinus the discursive individual soul, once it performs at its utmost the intellectual activity, is also in a position to contemplate the One, as the separate Intellect does. This is admittedly different from the beatific vision mentioned in the Arabic adaptation, but is not a complete misunderstanding of Plotinus's point.

to Plato, whose thoroughness on this point he affirms to be unprecedented. Better than anyone else, Plato has explained why the soul enters this world (a sentence that comes from Plotinus) and how soul will "return to her own world, the true, the first world" (ed. Badawī, 23.15–16; trans. Lewis 1959, 229)—a sentence that does not come from Plotinus, but is added in the Arabic.

If anyone levels the objection that Plato's statements are inconsistent, because in some of his writings he condemns the soul's union with body while in others this union counts as the fulfillment of God's decree, the "Allegorist" declares that Plato's behavior is meant to incite the reader into going beyond the face value of these statements. All this comes from Plotinus (IV 8[6], 1.28–29), and so it is also for the assessment of the crucial role of the *Timaeus*. For Plotinus, in this dialogue one can find not only Plato's doctrine about body and soul, but also Plato's answer to the cosmological question as a whole, namely whether or not the divine Intellect acted well in producing the world of becoming (IV 8[6], 2.1–8). At this point, the Arabic text parts company with the treatise *On the Descent of the Soul into the Bodies*, and a long section begins that has no counterpart in the Greek text. The "Allegorist" wears the cloak of the exegete of Plato's theological doctrine.

> We intend to begin by giving the view of this surpassing and sublime man on these things we have mentioned. We say that when the sublime Plato saw that the mass of philosophers were at fault in their description of the essences, for when they wished to know about the true essences they sought them in this sensible world, because they rejected intelligible things and turned to the sensible world alone, wishing to attain by sense-perception all things, both the transitory and the eternally abiding . . . he pitied them . . . and guided them to the road that would bring them to the truth of things. He distinguished between mind and sense-perception and between the nature of the essences and the sensible things. He established that the true essences were everlasting, not changing their state, and that the sensible things were transitory, falling under genesis and corruption. When he had completed this distinction he began by saying "the cause of the true essences, which are bodiless, and of the sensible things, which have bodies, is one and the same, and that is the first true essence," meaning by that the Creator, the Maker. (ps.-*Theol. Ar.*, I, ed. Badawī, 25.15–26.8; trans. Lewis 1959, 231)

This passage, with its deliberate echo of the Aristotelian history of philosophy as a progress from the materialistic beginnings toward a fully fledged doctrine of the true causes (*Metaph.* A.3, 983b6–11), with its distinction between the mass of the philosophers liable to error and the leading ones who guide others toward truth, and with the final move of crediting Plato with the doctrine of creation, is of great importance for the development of Arabic-Islamic philosophy. Even more important is the fact that the exegete, "Aristotle," openly endorses the master's ideas, namely "Plato's" ones, presenting creation as a doctrine shared by both: note that the elucidation that the "first true essence" (*al-anniyya al-ūlā al-ḥaqq*) is "the Creator, the Maker" (*al-bāriʾ al-khāliq*) is provided by "Aristotle" himself. It is still "Aristotle" who extols "Plato" for having taught the same doctrine that he himself had announced at the beginning of his *Theology*, namely the existence of Intellect and Soul as the principles that convey the creative power of the First Cause:

> Then he said: "This world is compounded of matter and form. What informed matter was a nature more exalted than matter and superior to it, viz. the intellectual soul. It was only by the power of the sublime mind within the soul that she came to inform matter. Mind came to give the soul the power to inform matter only by virtue of the first essence, which is the cause of the other essences, those of mind, of soul and of matter, and all natural things. Only because of the First Agent did the sensible things become beautiful and splendid, but this action took place only through the medium of mind and soul." Then he said: "It is the true first essence that pours forth life, first upon mind, then upon soul, then upon the natural things, this being the Creator, who is absolute good." How well and how rightly does this philosopher describe the Creator when he says "He created mind, soul and nature and all things else." (ps.-*Theol. Ar.*, ed. Badawī, I, 26.16–27.8; trans. Lewis 1959, 231)

The "Allegorist" credits Plato with the (admittedly Aristotelian) hylomorphic doctrine and sides with him in the assessment of the emanation of divine power through the medium of the Intellect and the cosmic Soul. This account of divine causality culminates in the claim that the First Agent, the First Essence, and the Pure Good are one and the same thing: the Creator. The enthusiastic comment on "Plato's" doctrine—"How well and how rightly . . ."—paves the way for "Aristotle" to turn into the learned disciple who warrants for the correct interpretation of the master's doctrine. Once established the harmony between his own views and "Plato's," he sets for himself the task of avoiding a possible misunderstanding: since creation is an "action" that "took place through the medium of mind and soul," and since it is described as a sequence of deeds ("*first* upon mind, *then* upon soul, *then* upon the natural things"), one may infer that God's creation was performed at a given time, as suggested also by the narrative of the *Timaeus*—a highly problematic conclusion indeed, since in this way God himself seems to be submitted to time. But "Aristotle" explains that the sequence is only due to the limitations of language (*lafẓ*), because language cannot convey the notion of priority if not through time:

> But whoever hears the philosopher's words must not take them literally (*ilā lafẓihi*) and imagine that the Creator fashioned the creation in time. If anyone imagines that of him from his [i.e., Plato's] mode of expression, he did but so express himself through wishing to follow the custom of the ancients. The ancients were compelled to mention time in connection with the beginning of creation because they wanted to describe the genesis of things, and they were compelled to introduce time into their description of genesis and into their description of the creation—which was not in time at all—in order to distinguish between the exalted first causes and the lowly secondary causes. The reason is that when a man wishes to elucidate and recognize cause he is compelled to mention time, since the cause is bound to be prior to

> its effect, and one imagines that priority means time and that every agent performs his action in time. But it is not so; not every agent performs his action in time, nor is every cause prior to its effect in time. If you wish to know whether this act is temporal or not, consider the agent: if he be subject to time then is the act subject to time, inevitably, and if the cause is temporal so too is the effect. The agent and the cause indicate the nature of the act and the effect, if they be subject to time or not subject to it. (ps.-*Theol. Ar.*, ed. Badawī, I, 27.8–28.3; trans. Lewis 1959, 231)

This passage sheds light on the scope of this crucial section of the ps.-*Theology*. Should the exegesis of "Plato's" utterances be intended to reconcile the doctrine of the philosophers with the Qurʾān, it would surprisingly miss the mark: indeed, a literal interpretation of the *Timaeus* would fit better with the narratives of creation that feature in the sacred book of Islam, and the emphasis laid here on the conventional nature of the accounts that include time would rather fan the flames of a controversy between philosophy and religion than warrant for the Islamic orthodoxy of Greek thought. Thus, the scope of "Aristotle" in providing the key to the correct interpretation of "Plato's" doctrine of creation cannot be apologetic. Rather, "Aristotle's" account is meant to grant a firm footing to the theory of the "harmony between Plato and Aristotle" on the crucial issue of the causality of the First Principle, a move that presupposes the awareness of the objections against the *Timaeus* raised by Aristotle in the *De Caelo*: one should not forget that the *De Caelo* was known in the circle of al-Kindī, where the ps.-*Theology* was born (Endress 1997), and to some extent also the *Timaeus* was (Arnzen 2012).

The interpretation of divine causality as an action that, prima facie similar to a process, in reality is performed in no time is typically Neoplatonic, but what is most interesting here is the fact "Aristotle's" account depends upon Philoponus's reply to Proclus. In his *De Aeternitate mundi* Philoponus came to grips with Proclus's eternalist arguments, listed in a work (*Eighteenth Arguments on the Eternity of the Cosmos*) that has come down to us in Greek only through Philoponus's quotations. One of these arguments inferred from the changeless nature of the divine is the impossibility for the Demiurge to produce anything new. In purely Neoplatonic vein, Philoponus retorted that the suprasensible principles always operate according to their own nature, not according to the nature of the lower realities they produce; hence, the Demiurge "operates without subdivision on divisible things, in unitary way on multiple things, and always in the same way on changeable things" (*De Aet. mundi*, ed. Rabe 1899, 617.15–18). The *De Aeternitate mundi* was known to al-Kindī and in his circle (Walzer 1957, 190–96; Endress 1973, 15–17; Ivry 1974, 144–62; Davidson 1987, 106–15; Hasnaoui 1994), and it is revealing to see the creation described in the ps.-*Theology* as an action whose quality is assigned by the agent, performed in no time because the agent is above time. This account, clearly inspired by Philoponus, is put in the mouth of the "Allegorist"—"Aristotle"—and emphasized as a point made by "Plato." When, later on, the ps.-*Theology* is quoted in the *Harmonization of the Two Opinions of the Two Sages, Plato the Divine and Aristotle*, its author will insist on the fact that the philosophers alone can provide good arguments for creation out of nothing. If one relies on the symbolic language of the Scripture, one is left with the idea of production out of something preexistent—water, foam, smoke, clay—and this does not do justice to God's absolute power to create out of nothing. Only philosophy disposes satisfactorily of the anthropomorphic narratives that misrepresent God's action as if it were that of a craftsman in need of a preexistent matter (ed. Martini Bonadeo, 63.16–64.6 and 66.1–67.3; English trans. Butterworth 2001, 154–57). Also al-Fārābī's definition of creation, in the *Opinions of the Inhabitants of the Perfect State* (ed. Walzer 1985, 92.8–10), as an act accomplished without any movement, without instruments, without any change whatsoever, testifies to the adoption of the Neoplatonic notion of causality, with which the *falāsifa* were acquainted through the texts produced within the circle of al-Kindī: the ps.-*Theology* and the *Liber de Causis*.

The ps.-*Theology* shows an overarching concern with the issue of God's causality. Very often we can read in it adaptations of Plotinus's accounts of intelligible causality, which pave the way for the well-known formulas of the *Liber de Causis* about the First Principle as that pure Being which creates by its own being, without instruments, with no change, and in no time. This topic appears with some emphasis at the very end of the ps.-*Theology*. Chapter 10, the last one, consists of three blocks of Plotinian writings: the short treatise V 2[11], *On the Origin and Order of the Beings Which Come after the First*; a long section from the treatise VI 7[38], *How the Multitude of the Forms Came into Being, and on the Good*; finally, a section from the treatise V 8[31], *On the Intelligible Beauty*. Here Plotinus argues against the literal interpretation of the *Timaeus*, which may lead to the conclusion, widespread in Gnostic circles, that the principle that fashioned this universe operated like a craftsman, making first the choice whether to produce an artifact or not, then planning his deeds, then again himself doing the job step by step. This counts for Plotinus as a complete misunderstanding of the *Timaeus*, as he repeats time and again in his treatises; in particular, in V 8[31] he protests against those who imagine that the demiurgic "reasoning" about the cosmos can be taken at its face value (V 8[31], 7.1–17). In the final part of the ps.-*Theology*, this doctrine is endorsed and adapted on two points: what Plotinus says about the divine Intellect is referred to the First Cause itself, and the production of the universe is understood as creation. Once again, in what follows the italics indicate the sentences taken almost literally from the Greek; the rest is Arabic adaptation.

> *Who will not wonder at the power of that noble and divine substance, that it originated things without reflection or investigation of their causes* but originated them by the mere fact of its being? Its being is the cause of the causes and therefore its being *has no need*, in originating things, *of investigating* their causes, *or of cunning* in bringing them well into existence and perfection, because it is the cause of causes, as we said above, being self-sufficient without need of any cause or contemplation or investigation. *We are going to cite an example supporting our description, for this statement of ours*. We say that *the accounts of the ancients are unanimous, that this universe did not come into being by its own act* or by chance, but came from a skilful and surpassing craftsman. But we must investigate his fashioning of this universe: *whether the craftsman first reflected*, when he wished to fashion it, *and thought within himself that first he must create an earth standing in the middle of the universe, then after that water, to*

> *be above the earth*, then create air and put it above the water, then create fire and put it above the air, *then create a heaven* and put it above the fire, surrounding all things, *then create animals with various forms suited to each creature of them, and make their members, internal and external*, following the description they follow, suited to their functions; *so he formed the things in his mind* and reflected over the perfection of his knowledge, *then began creating the works of creation* one by one, in the way he previously reflected and thought. No one must imagine that this description applies to the wise Creator, for that is absurd and impossible and inappropriate to that perfect, surpassing and noble substance. (ps.-*Theol. Ar.*, X, ed. Badawī, 161.16–162.3; trans. Lewis 1959, 393)

In his interpretation of the narrative of the *Timaeus*, Plotinus did not limit himself to following the path laid out in the Platonic school, which consisted in vindicating the didascalic nature of an account that deploys a logical structure in a chronological sequence. He also interpreted this narrative in the light of his own understanding of the theory of Ideas. For Plotinus, the philosophical truth of Plato's doctrine lies in that, in spite of Aristotle's irony (*De Gen. et corr.* II 9, 335 b 9–16; cf. *Metaph.* A.9, 991b3–9), it is precisely *because* Forms are not involved in the process of producing something that they are causes. Their causality consists in being each of them what it is: the intelligible principle that assigns the rationale behind the processes whose outcome is a thing. In order to "produce" the logical structure of a thing, Form must "do" nothing if not being what it is: the model whose instantiation is the logical structure of a given being. This philosophical doctrine, which lies in the background of images like the emanation of heat from fire, is adopted in the ps.-*Theology* as the most natural explanation of the way in which "the wise Creator" operates, and it is "Aristotle" who propounds this explanation of Plato's doctrine of creation. The "cause of the causes" produces by the mere fact of its being—*bi-anniyyatihi faqaṭ, per esse suum tantum*: a formulaic expression that will dominate the accounts of creation as a changeless and timeless emanation of the causal power of the First Principle, from al-Fārābī to Avicenna and beyond.

> He does not need any instrument in the origination of things because he is the cause of instruments, it being he that originated them, and in what he originates he needs nothing of his origination. Now that the unsoundness and impossibility of this doctrine are made plain, we say that there is, between him and his creation, no intermediate thing on which he reflects and the help of which he seeks, but that he originated things by the mere fact of its being. (ps.-*Theology*, X, ed. Badawī, 163.4–8; trans. Lewis 1959, 395)

In the *Book of the Exposition by Aristotle on the Pure Good*, which after the translation into Latin by Gerard of Cremona (d. 1187) will be known as the *Liber de Causis*, creation by the mere fact of the Creator's being is assessed as follows:

> Therefore, let us return and say that every agent that acts through its being alone is neither a connecting link nor another mediating thing. The connecting link between

> an agent and its effect is nothing but an addition to being, as when an agent and its effect are through an instrument and [the agent] does not act through its being. . . . But an agent [in which] there is no connecting link at all between itself and its effect is a true agent and a true ruler. (*Liber de Causis* 19, ed. Bardenhewer 1882, 96.6–8; trans. Taylor et al. 1996, 120–21)

The uniqueness of the causality of the First Principle consists, in the Arabic Plotinus, precisely in that it operates without anything preëxistent, only out of its being and because of its absolute self-sufficiency: this is why it is "the cause of the causes." The First Cause alone is capable of acting in this way. Unlike it, the suprasensible principles that transmit the causal power of the First Cause to visible things—Intellect and the cosmic Soul—operate only because their causality is included in and supported by this power. Another passage of the ps.-*Theology* with no counterpart in the Greek, this too located in the last chapter, conveys the views of the author of the adaptation of Plotinus. These ideas will have a long-lasting influence on Arabic-Islamic philosophy:

> You must understand that mind and soul and the other intelligible things are from the first originator, not passing away or disappearing, on account of their originating from the first cause without intermediary, whereas nature and sense-perception and the other natural things perish and fall under corruption because they are effects of causes that are caused, that is, of the mind through the medium of the soul. But of the natural things one has a longer duration than the others, being the most lasting: that depends on the remoteness of the thing from its cause, or its proximity, and on the multitude or paucity of causes in it: for when the causes of the thing are few its duration is longer, and if its causes are many the thing is of shorter duration. We must understand that natural things are linked one to another: when one of them passes away it comes to its neighbour until it reaches the heavenly bodies, then soul, then mind. All things are fixed in mind and mind is fixed in the first cause, and the first cause is the beginning and end of all things: from it do they originate and to it is their returning, as we have often said. (ps.-*Theology*, X, ed. Badawī, 138.16–139.5; trans. Lewis 1959, 297)

The great chain of being has its beginning in the First Principle, the One, the Pure Being and Pure Good: every degree depends on it and its power reaches the sublunar beings through the medium of Intellect and Soul. In the first chapter "Aristotle" had amplified Plotinus's sentence about the descent of the soul by a sentence of his own, concerning its return to the realm of the incorporeal, eternal principles. Here, toward the end of the ps.-*Theology*, we find another amplification in the same vein. Plotinus was dealing with the destiny of the soul after the end of the body it gives life to (V 2[11], 2.21–23), and the passage quoted above presents once again the cosmic hierarchy of the principles: the First Cause, Intellect, and Soul. At the beginning of the ps.-*Theology* as well as here, toward the end, the description of the chain of being is dominated by the pattern of the double journey of the soul, the way down along the necessary declension of the degrees of being, and the way back toward its homeland. What will become, in Avicenna's phrasing, the "provenance and destination" is one of the most influential topics created in the ps.-*Theology*.

> This treatise of mine contains the fruit of two great sciences, one of which is characterized by being about metaphysical, and the other physical, matters. The fruit of the science dealing with metaphysical matters is that part of it known as theology (*Uthūlūjiyyā*), which treats [the subjects of] Lordship, the first principle, and the relationship which beings bear to it according to their rank. The fruit of the science dealing with physical matters is the knowledge that the human soul survives and that it has a Destination. (Avicenna, *The Provenance and Destination*, introduction, trans. Gutas 1988, 31)

The literary traces of the ps.-*Theology* can be detected in many works of classical and postclassical Arabic philosophy. In addition to the authors and texts mentioned above, the ps.-*Theology* is alluded to or quoted by al-ʿĀmirī (*Book on the Afterlife*, ed. Rowson 1984, V, 88–95; VII, 102–3; XV, 140–41), by Miskawayh (*al-Fawz al-aṣghar*, ed. ʿUḍayma 1987, 99.9–12), by Avicenna, who has commented upon it (Badawī 1947, 37–74 and Vajda 1951), by ʿAbd al-Laṭīf al-Baghdādī (*Book on the Science of Metaphysics*, Badawī 1955, 209–40, and Martini Bonadeo 2013), and in the *Ishrāqī* tradition (Rizvi 2007). The Safavid theologians of the schools of Shiraz and Isfahan show a renewed interest for the basic works of *falsafa*, tracing back to the age of the translations: among them, the ps.-*Theology* (Endress 2001, Di Branco 2014), as is made evident from Mullā Ṣadrā's *Four Journeys*; Saʿīd Qummī (d. 1102/1691) wrote a commentary on the ps.-*Theology* (Āshtiyānī 1978). The topic of the ultimate provenance of the soul from the First Principle and of its return to it through the conjunction with the intelligible realm is the most pervasive of the doctrines of the ps.-*Theology*, permeating as it does also the thought of philosophers who do not exhibit any direct knowledge of the Arabic Plotinus.

References

Abū Rīda, M. ʿA. (ed.). 1950. *Rasāʾil al-Kindī al-falsafiyya*. 2 vols. Cairo: Dār al-fikr al-ʿarabī. 2nd ed. 1978.

Adamson, P. 2007. *Al-Kindi*. Oxford: Oxford University Press.

ʿAjam, R. 1994 (ed.). ʿAlī ibn Zayd al-Bayhaqī, *Tatimmat Ṣiwān al-ḥikma*. Beirut: Dār al-fikr al-islāmī.

Altmann, A. 1963. "The Delphic Maxim in Medieval Islam and Judaism." In *Biblical and Other Studies*, vol. 1. Cambridge, MA: Harvard University Press, 196–232. Reprinted in *Studies in Religious Philosophy and Mysticism* (Ithaca, NY: Cornell University Press, 1969).

Aouad, M. 1989. "La *Théologie d'Aristote* et autres textes du *Plotinus Arabus*." In *Dictionnaire des philosophes antiques*, vol. 1, under the direction of R. Goulet. Paris: CNRS Éditions, 541–90.

Armstrong, A. H. (trans.) 1984. *Plotinus*. Vol. 4. Cambridge, MA: Harvard University Press; London: W. Heinemann.

Arnzen, R. 2012. "Plato's *Timaeus* in the Arabic Tradition: Legend—Testimonies—Fragments." In *Il Timeo: Esegesi greche, arabe, latine*, ed. F. Celia and A. Ulacco. Pisa: Pisa University Press, 181–267.

Āshtiyānī, J. (ed.) 1978. *Uthūlujiyā, taʾlīf Aflūṭīn. Tarjama-i Ibn Nāʿima al-Ḥimṣī, bā-taʿliqāt qāḍī Saʿīd Qummī*. Tehran: Intishārāt-i Anjuman-i Shāhanshāhī-i Falsafa-i Īrān.

Badawī, ʿA. (ed.) 1947. *Arisṭū ʿinda l-ʿArab. Dirāsāt wa-nuṣūṣ ghayr manshūra*. Cairo: Maktabat al-nahḍa al-miṣriyya.

Badawī, ʿA. (ed.) 1952. *Manṭiq Arisṭū*. Vol. 3. Cairo: Dār al-kutub al-miṣriyya.

Badawī, ʿA. (ed.) 1955. *Aflūṭīn ʿinda l-ʿarab. Plotinus apud Arabes: Theologia Aristotelis et fragmenta quae supersunt*. Cairo: Maktabat al-nahḍa al-miṣriyya. Reprinted Cairo: Dār al-nahḍa al-miṣriyya, 1966.

Bardenhewer, O. (ed.) 1882. Aristotle, *Liber de Causis*. Freiburg: Herder'sche Verlagshandlung.

Baumstark, A. 1902. "Zur Vorgeschichte der arabischen *Theologie des Aristoteles*." *Oriens Christianus* 2: 187–91.

Borisov, A. [1942] 2002. "Problems in the Study of the *Theology of Aristotle*." In *Materialy i issledovaniia po istorii Neoplatonizma na srednevekovom Vostoke* [*Materials and Studies on the History of Neoplatonism in the Medieval East*], ed. K. B. Starkova. St. Petersburg: DB, 14–116.

Brock, S. 2007. "A Syriac Intermediary for the Arabic *Theology of Aristotle*? In Search of a Chimera." In *The Libraries of the Neoplatonists*, ed. C. D'Ancona. Leiden: Brill, 293–306.

Bucur, C., and B. G. Bucur. 2006. "'The Place of Splendor and Light': Observations on the Paraphrasing of *Enn* 4.8.1 in the *Theology of Aristotle*." *Le Muséon* 119: 271–92.

Butterworth, C., trans. 2001. Abū Naṣr al-Fārābī, *Alfarabi: The Political Writings. "Selected Aphorisms" and Other Texts*. Ithaca, NY: Cornell University Press.

D'Ancona, C. 2008. "Degrees of Abstraction in Avicenna. How to Combine Aristotle's *De Anima* and the *Enneads*." In *Theories of Perception in Medieval and Early Modern Philosophy*, Ed. S. Knuuttila and P. Karkaineen. New York: Springer, 47–71.

D'Ancona, C. 2011. "La *Teologia* neoplatonica di 'Aristotele' e gli inizi della filosofia arabo-musulmana." In *Entre Orient et Occident: La philosophie et la science gréco-romaines dans le monde arabe. 57e Entretiens sur l'Antiquité Classique*, ed. R. Goulet and U. Rudolph. Vandœuvres, Geneva: Fondation Hardt, 135–90.

D'Ancona, C. 2012. "The Textual Tradition of the Arabic Plotinus: The *Theology of Aristotle*, Its *ruʾūs al-masāʾil*, and the Greek Model of the Arabic Version." In *The Letter before the Spirit: The Importance of Text Editions for the Study of the Reception of Aristotle*, ed. A. M. I. van Oppenraay and R. Fontaine. Leiden: Brill, 37–71.

D'Ancona, C., P. Bettiolo, et al. (ed. and trans.) 2003. *Plotino, La discesa dell'anima nei corpi (Enn. IV 8[6]. Plotiniana Arabica (pseudo-Teologia di Aristotele, capitoli 1 e 7; "Detti del Sapiente Greco")*. Padova: Il Poligrafo.

Davidson, H. A. 1987. *Proofs for Eternity, Creation and the Existence of God in Medieval Islamic and Jewish Philosophy*. New York: Oxford University Press.

De Smet, D. 2012. *La philosophie ismaélienne: Un ésotérisme chiite entre néoplatonisme et gnose*. Paris: Cerf.

Di Branco, M. (2014). "The 'Perfect King' and his Philosophers. Religion and Graeco-Arabic Philosophy in Safavid Iran: The Case of the Uṯūlūǧiyā." *Studia graeco-arabica* 4: 191-218.

Dieterici, F. (ed.) 1882. *Die sogenannte Theologie des Aristoteles aus arabischen Handschriften zum ersten Mal herausgegeben*. Leipzig: J. C. Hinrichs'sche Buchhandlung. Reprinted Amsterdam: Rodopi, 1965.

Dieterici, F. (trans.) 1883. *Die sogenannte Theologie des Aristoteles aus dem Arabischen übersetzt und mit Anmerkungen versehen*. Leipzig: J. C. Hinrichs'sche Buchhandlung. Reprinted Reinheim: Druckerei Lokay, n.d.

Endress, G. 1966. *Die arabischen Übersetzungen von Aristoteles' Schrift "De Caelo"*. PhD dissertation, Frankfurt University.

Endress, G. (ed. and trans.) 1973. *Proclus Arabus. Zwanzig Abschnitte aus der Institutio Theologica in arabischer Übersetzung*. Wiesbaden/Beirut: Imprimerie Catholique.

Endress, G. 1997. "The Circle of al-Kindī. Early Arabic Translations from the Greek and the Rise of Islamic Philosophy." In *The Ancient Tradition in Christian and Islamic Hellenism: Studies on the Transmission of Greek Philosophy and Sciences Dedicated to H. J. Drossaart Lulofs on His Ninetieth Birthday*, ed. G. Endress and R. Kruk. Leiden: CNWS School, 43–76.

Endress, G. 2000. "The New and Improved Platonic Theology: *Proclus Arabus* and Arabic Islamic Philosophy." In *Proclus et la théologie platonicienne: Actes du Colloque International de Louvain (13–16 mai 1998) en l'honneur de H. D. Saffrey et L. G. Westerink*, ed. A. P. Segonds and C. Steel. Leuven: Leuven University Press; Paris: Les Belles Lettres, 553–70.

Endress, G. 2001. "Philosophische Ein-Band-Bibliotheken aus Isfahan." *Oriens* 36: 10–58.

Endress, G. 2007. "Building the Library of Arabic Philosophy: Platonism and Aristotelianism in the Sources of al-Kindī." In *The Libraries of the Neoplatonists: Proceedings of the Meeting of the European Science Foundation Network "Late Antiquity and Arabic Thought"*, ed. C. D'Ancona. Leiden: Brill, 319–50.

Endress, G. 2008. "L'armonia delle tesi di Platone e Aristotele in al-Fārābī e lo sviluppo della sua filosofia." Preface to Abū Naṣr al-Fārābī, *L'armonia delle opinioni dei due sapienti, il divino Platone e Aristotele*, ed. and trans. C. Martini Bonadeo. Pisa: Plus.

Endress, G. 2012. "Höfischer Stil und wissenschaftliche Rhetorik: Al-Kindī als Epistolograph." In *Islamic Philosophy, Science, Culture, and Religion: Studies in Honor of Dimitri Gutas*, ed. F. Opwis and D. Reisman. Leiden: Brill, 289–306.

Fabricius, J. 1716. *Bibliotheca Graeca*. Vol. 3. Hamburg: Christiani Liebezeit.

Fenton, P. 1986. "The Arabic and Hebrew Versions of the *Theology of Aristotle*." In *Pseudo-Aristotle in the Middle Ages: The Theology and Other Texts*, ed. J. Kraye, W. F. Ryan, and C.-B. Schmitt. London: Warburg Institute, 241–64.

Gauthier, L, ed. 1981. Muḥammad ibn ʿAbd al-Malik Ibn Ṭufayl, *Ḥayy bin Yaqẓān*. Beirut: Kitāba.

Geoffroy, M. 2002. "La tradition arabe du Περὶ νοῦ d'Alexandre d'Aphrodise et les origines de la théorie farabienne des quatre degrés de l'intellect." In *Aristotele e Alessandro di Afrodisia nella tradizione araba*, ed. C. D'Ancona and G. Serra. Padova: Il Poligrafo, 191–231.

Ghālib, M. (ed.) 1984. *Al-Risāla al-jāmiʿa. Tāj rasāʾil ikhwān al-safāʾ wa-khullān al-wafāʾ*. Beirut: Dār al-Andalus.

Gleede, B. 2012. "*Creatio ex nihilo*: A Genuinely Philosophical Insight Derived from Plato and Aristotle? Some Notes on the *Treatise on the Harmony between the Two Sages*." *Arabic Sciences and Philosophy* 22: 91–117.

Gutas, D. 1988. *Avicenna and the Aristotelian Tradition: Introduction to Reading Avicenna's Philosophical Works*. Leiden: Brill.

Hämeen-Anttila, J. 2006. *The Last Pagans of Iraq: Ibn Washiyya and His Nabatean Agriculture*. Leiden: Brill.

Hansberger, R. 2011. "Plotinus Arabus Rides Again." *Arabic Sciences and Philosophy* 21: 57–84.

Hasnaoui, A. 1994. "Alexandre d'Aphrodise *vs* Jean Philopon: Notes sur quelques traités d'Alexandre 'perdus' en grec, conservés en arabe." *Arabic Sciences and Philosophy* 4: 53–109.

Ibn al-Nadīm, *Kitāb al-Fihrist*, ed. R. Tajaddud, Tehran 1971, 1973[3]

Ibn al-Nadīm, *Kitāb al-Fihrist*, mit Anmerkungen hrsg. von G. Flügel, I - II (= Rödiger - Müller), Leipzig 1871-1872.

Ivry, A. L., trans. 1974. *Al-Kindī's Metaphysics: A Translation of Yaʿqūb ibn Isḥāq al-Kindī's Treatise "On First Philosophy" (fī al-Falsafah al-Ulā) with Introduction and Commentary*. Albany: SUNY Press.

Kraus, P. 1940–41. "Plotin chez les Arabes: Remarques sur un nouveau fragment de la paraphrase arabe des *Ennéades*." *Bulletin de l'Institut d'Égypte* 23: 263–95.
Lewis, G. L. 1957. Review of Badawī, *Aflūṭīn ʿinda l-ʿarab*, 1955. *Oriens* 10: 395–98.
Lewis, G. L., trans. 1959. Plotinus, *Opera*. Vol. 2: *Enneades IV–V*. Ed. P. Henry and H.-R. Schwyzer. Paris: Desclée de Brouwer.
Mariën, B. 1973. "Bibliografia critica degli studi plotiniani con rassegna delle loro recensioni." In Plotinus, *Enneadi: Prima versione integra e commentario critico di V. Cilento*, vol. 3. Bari: Laterza, 391–622.
Martini Bonadeo, C., ed. and trans. 2008. Abū Naṣr al-Fārābī, *L'armonia delle opinioni dei due sapienti, il divino Platone e Aristotele*. Pisa: Plus.
Martini Bonadeo, C. 2013. *ʿAbd al-Laṭīf al-Baghdādī's Philosophical Journey: From Aristotle's Metaphysics to the Metaphysical Science*. Leiden: Brill.
Mattila, J. 2007. "Ibn Waḥshiyya on the Soul: Neoplatonic Soul Doctrine and the Treatise on the Soul Contained in the *Nabatean Agriculture*." *Studia Orientalia* 101: 103–55.
Munk, S. 1959. *Mélanges de philosophie juive et arabe*. Paris: Franck. Reprinted Paris: Vrin, 1988.
Pines, S. 1954. "La longue recension de la *Théologie d'Aristote* dans ses rapports avec la doctrine ismaélienne." *Revue des Études Islamiques* 22: 7–20.
Rabe, H., ed. 1899. John Philoponus, *De Aeternitate mundi contra Proclum*. Leipzig: Teubner.
Rashed, M. 2009. "On the Authorship of the Treatise *On the Harmonization of the Opinions of the Two Sages* Attributed to al-Fārābī." *Arabic Sciences and Philosophy* 19: 43–82.
Rashed, R., and J. Jolivet, (ed. and trans.) 1999. *Oeuvres philosophiques et scientifiques d'al-Kindî*. Vol. 2: *Métaphysique et cosmologie*. Leiden: Brill.
Rizvi, S. 2007. "(Neo)Platonism Revived in the Light of the Imams: Qadi Sa'id al-Qummi (d. AH 1107/AD 1696) and His Reception of the *Theologia Aristotelis*." In *Classical Arabic Philosophy: Sources and Reception*, ed. P. Adamson. London: Warburg Institute, 176–207.
Rose, V. 1883. "Review of F. Dieterici, *Die sogenannte Theologie des Aristoteles aus dem Arabischen übersetzt und mit Anmerkungen versehen*." *Deutsche Literaturzeitung für Kritik der internationalen Wissenschaft* 4: cols. 843–46.
Rosenthal, F. 1942. "Al-Kindī als Literat." *Orientalia* 2: 262–88.
Rosenthal, F. 1952–55. "Aš-Šayḫ al-Yūnānī and the Arabic Plotinus Source." *Orientalia* 21 (1952): 461–92; 22 (1953): 370–400; 24 (1955): 42–65. Reprinted in *Greek Philosophy in the Arab World: A Collection of Essays* (London: Variorum, 1990).
Rosenthal, F. 1955. "From Arabic Books and Manuscripts. V: A One-Volume Library of Arabic Philosophical and Scientific Texts in Istanbul." *Journal of the American Oriental Society* 75: 14–23.
Rosenthal, F. 1974. "Plotinus in Islam: The Power of Anonymity." In *Plotino e il Neoplatonismo in Oriente e in Occidente: Atti del convegno internazionale Roma, 5–9 ottobre 1970*. Rome: Accademia Nazionale dei Lincei, 437–46. Reprinted in *Greek Philosophy in the Arab World: A Collection of Essays* (London: Variorum, 1990).
Rowson, E. K. 1984. "An Unpublished Work by al-ʿĀmirī and the Date of the Arabic *De Causis*." *Journal of the American Oriental Society* 104: 193–99.
Salinger, G. G. 1971. "Neoplatonic Passages in the *Nabatean Agriculture*, Work of the Tenth Century Ascribed to b. Waḥshīya." In *Proceedings of the Twenty-Seventh International Congress of Orientalists (Ann Arbor, Michigan, 13th–19th August 1967)*, ed. D. Sinor. Wiesbaden: Harrassowitz, 233–34.
Schwyzer, H.-R. 1941. "Die pseudoaristotelische *Theologie* und die Plotin-Ausgabe des Porphyrios." *Rheinisches Museum* 90: 216–36.

Stern, S. M. 1960–61. "Ibn Ḥasday's Neoplatonist: A Neoplatonist Treatise and Its Influence on Isaac Israeli and the Longer Version of the *Theology of Aristotle*." *Oriens* 13: 58–120.

Stern, S. M. 1962. "The First in Thought Is the Last in Action: The History of a Saying Attributed to Aristotle." *Journal of Semitic Studies* 7: 234–52.

Taylor, R. C., V. A. Guagliardo, and C. R. Hess, trans. 1996. Thomas Aquinas, *Commentary on the Book of Causes*. Washington, DC: Catholic University of America Press.

Taylor, T. 1812. *A Dissertation on the Philosophy of Aristotle in Four Books*. London: n.p. Reprinted Kessinger, 2003.

Treiger, A. 2007. "Andrei Iakovlevič Borisov (1903–1942) and His Studies of Medieval Arabic Philosophy." *Arabic Sciences and Philosophy* 17: 159–95.

ʿUḍayma, S. (ed.) 1987. Miskawayh, *Kitāb al-fawz al-aṣghar*. Translated into French by R. Arnaldez. Tunis: Dār al-ʿarabiyya li-l-kitāb.

Vajda, G. 1951. "Les notes d'Avicenne sur la *Théologie d'Aristote*." *Revue Thomiste* 59: 346–406.

van Ess, J. 1966. "Über einige neue Fragmente des Alexander von Aphrodisias und des Proklos in arabischer Übersetzung." *Der Islam* 42: 148–68.

Wakelnig, E. (ed. and trans.) 2014. *A Philosophy Reader from the Circle of Miskawayh* edited and translated by E. Wakelnig, Cambridge U. P., Cambridge 2014.

Walzer, R. 1957. "New Studies on al-Kindī." *Oriens* 10: 203–52. Reprinted in *Greek into Arabic: Essays in Islamic Philosophy* (Oxford: Cassirer 1962), 175–205.

Walzer, R, trans. 1985. Abū Naṣr al-Fārābī, *On the Perfect State (Mabādi' ārā' ahl al-madīna al-fāḍilah*. Chicago: Great Books of the Islamic World.

Zimmermann, F. W. 1986. "The Origins of the So-Called *Theology of Aristotle*." In *Pseudo-Aristotle in the Middle Ages: The Theology and Other Texts*, ed. J. Kraye, W. F. Ryan, and C. B. Schmitt. London: The Warburg Institute, 11–240.

CHAPTER 2

THE RISE OF *FALSAFA*

Al-Kindī (d. 873), *On First Philosophy*

EMMA GANNAGÉ

Abū Yūsuf Yaʿqūb b. Isḥāq al-Kindī (ca. 185/801–ca. 252/870), "the philosopher of the Arabs" as the biographical tradition likes to call him, was raised in Kufa, where his father was governor, to a family whose noble Arab lineage has been emphasized by all bibliographers. Very little is known about his life otherwise. According to the bio-bibliographical tradition, he held an important position at the caliph's court under al-Maʾmūn (198/813–218/833) and al-Muʿtaṣim (218/833–227/842), the latter appointing him as a preceptor for his son Aḥmad. However, he fell into disgrace under al-Mutawakkil (232/847–247/861), victim either of the intrigues of the Banū Mūsā, his rivals in court, or of his Muʿtazilī inclinations.

In a few words Dimitri Gutas encapsulated Kindī best as "a polymath and a universal scholar imbued with the spirit of encyclopedism which was characteristic of early 9th c. Bagdad and which was fostered by the translation movement" (Gutas 2004, 201). Indeed, al-Nadīm's *Fihrist* lists more than 250 titles under his name. They show an astonishing range of interests, reflecting all the sciences of his time. Around 50 of these (maybe more) seem to have been devoted to philosophy. *On First Philosophy* is the most important and the most famous of them.

2.1. Title

Our treatise bears the title *Kitāb al-Kindī ilā l-Muʿtaṣim bi-llāh Fī l-falsafa al-ūlā* (*Book of al-Kindī to al-Muʿtaṣim bi-llāh On First Philosophy*) in the only manuscript in which it has reached us (MS Istanbul, Aya Sofia 4832, ff. 196r–206r). Kindī himself refers to it by the same title, that is, *Fī l-falsafa al-ūlā*, in his treatise *On the Explanation of the Prostration of the Outermost Body and Its Obedience to God the Almighty and Exalted* (*Fī l-ibāna ʿan sujūd al-jirm al-aqṣā wa-ṭāʿatihi li-llāh ʿazza wa-jall*)

(*Prostration* hereafter) (*Œuvres*, 187.3; *Rasāʾil* 1:251.3), as well as in *On the Explanation of the Proximate Efficient Cause of Generation and Corruption* (*Fī l-ibāna ʿan al-ʿilla al-fāʿila al-qarība li-l-kawn wa-l-fasād*) (*Proximate* hereafter) (*Rasāʾil* 1:215.8), and in the prologue of his treatise *On the Great Art* (*Fī l-ṣināʿa al-ʿuẓmā*), namely his paraphrase of the first eight chapters of the first book of Ptolemy's *Almagest*, where it is referred to as *Kitāb fī l-falsafa al-ūlā al-dākhila* (Rosenthal 1956, 442; Kindī, *Ṣināʿa*, 127). However, the same treatise is listed by Nadīm (*Fihrist*, 1, 255) followed by Qifṭī (*Taʾrīkh*, 368 and Ibn Abī Uṣaybiʿa, *ʿUyūn*, 1, 206) as the *Book of First Philosophy, on What Is Above (beyond) Physics, and of Oneness* (*Kitāb al-Falsafa l-ūlā fīmā dūn al-ṭabīʿiyyāt wa-l-tawḥīd*).

Al-Falsafa al-ūlā or first philosophy is Aristotle's third designation of theoretical philosophy (*Metaph.* VI.1, 1026a29 ff. and XI.4, 1061b19 and 28 as well as 7, 1064a33–b3), and indeed Kindī treats first philosophy as a theology, though definitely not the theology of *Metaphysics* XII. As has been already noted, Aristotle's "theology" makes sense in the context of an eternal universe that is set in motion by a primary object of desire (see *Œuvres*, 4); whereas, as we will shortly see, Kindī shows in the second chapter that the universe is not eternal. It is created and has a creator. For Kindī then, first philosophy is the science of the first Cause, which is the "cause of time," as well as the science of the first Truth, which is the cause of every truth. Expressed in the prologue, this statement is echoed again in the conclusion of the treatise, which ends with the apparition of a first true One and first Creator, cause of the creation. The true One is thus the One God Almighty of the revealed religion, and the henology of chapter 4 ends with a description of the creative action of the One in which the philosophical theology of Neoplatonic inspiration is interwoven with Muslim religious and theological concepts in an intricate fabric that places Kindī at the crossroads of several traditions all at once (Jolivet 1984, 322–23; Ivry 1974, 14 ff.).

2.2. Scope and Structure

The *Book on First Philosophy* (*FPh* hereafter) is one of the longest of Kindī's treatises that have reached us, and yet it is incomplete. The fourth and last chapter ends with the mention of a sequel: "Let us complete this chapter (*fann*) and follow it up with what naturally comes after" (*Rasāʾil* 1:162.15; *Œuvres*, 99), and the colophon of the text makes this understanding clear when it says: "End of the *first part* (*al-juzʾ al-awwal*) of the book." Cross-references in Kindī's writings, as well as external evidence, corroborate the assumption of a larger work.

Aiming primarily to prove the oneness of God, the first and only surviving part of the treatise consists of four chapters that form a consistent unit (for a handy and yet detailed outline see *Œuvres*, 1–5). From the first page, which introduces the first Truth, cause of all truths, to the last page closing this first part with the apparition of a true One cause of the unity and the existence of all things, the treatise unfolds by following a very tight argument in which each step paves the way for the rest of the discussion. Despite some redundancy and an often obscure style, the treatise is organized in order to make room for a "henology" that unfurls progressively in chapters 3 and 4, leading to the thesis toward which the whole treatise seems to aim: the true One, who is the principle of unity and hence the principle of existence of all beings, on the one hand, and the absolutely transcendent God that can be approached only through a negative theology, on the other, are one and the same principle.

2.3. Sources, Program, and Method

Even though he is credited with having inaugurated the philosophical tradition in Islam, Kindī is part of a tradition to which he stakes a claim, as can be clearly demonstrated from the prologue of *FPh* (*Œuvres*, 13.15–22; *Rasāʾil* 1:103.4–11):

> We should not be ashamed of appreciating the truth and acquiring the truth wherever it comes from, even if it comes from remote races and different nations. For him who seeks the truth, nothing is worthier than the truth, and the truth is neither belittled nor demeaned by him who reports it or by him who brings it. Nobody is demeaned by the truth, but everybody is ennobled by the truth.
>
> We would do well—since we are striving to perfect our species and in this the truth resides—in this book to stick to our habits in all the subjects [we have dealt with]: to present what the ancients have dealt with completely, in the most straightforward and easiest way for those who will follow this path, and to complete what they did not deal with completely, following, in so doing, the custom of the language and the usages of the time, to the best of our ability.[1]

Indeed, Kindī's name is associated with the translation movement of scientific and philosophical works from Greek into Arabic (Hasnawi 1992, 655), though it is generally admitted that he did not know Greek. He was rather a "patron" around whom gravitated a group of translators, recognizable by a distinctive terminology and phraseology as well as by an often loose method of translation. Arabic versions of several of Aristotle's works have been produced in the so-called "circle" of Kindī as well as important fragments of Proclus and Philoponus often in the garb of Alexander of Aphrodisias (Endress 1973, 1997; Zimmermann 1986, 1994; Hasnawi 1994; for an annotated list of the main works translated in Kindī's circle see Endress 2007).

The ultimate aim of this activity of selecting, translating, paraphrasing, and rearranging has been clearly expressed in the lines quoted above and falls under more than one heading: (1) assimilation of Greek philosophy and science; (2) completing what the

[1] All translations of al-Kindī's texts are mine and based on *Œuvres*, unless otherwise specified. References to *Rasāʾil*, which I sometimes follow, are always mentioned along with it. For an English translation of al-Kindī's philosophical works see Adamson and Pormann 2012.

ancients did not achieve and hence developing Aristotle's metaphysic into a theology conveying a monotheistic and creationist interpretation of the Neoplatonic system that is compatible with the creed of the One and Unique God, the *tawḥīd* of Islam (Endress 1997, 54; Zimmermann 1986, 119), though there is no scholarly consensus as to the extent of the implication of al-Kindī as well as to the intentional reordering and misattribution (D'Ancona 2011, 1033); (3) creating a philosophical and scientific terminology in order to put the Greek philosophical and scientific corpus within the reach of his own community.

The breadth and depth of the activity of Kindī's circle as well as the wide array of sources translated will, not surprisingly, find a direct echo in Kindī's own work, not only in terms of doctrinal influence, but also in terms of method and style. Maybe more than any of his other works, *FPh* reflects the influences that have shaped the worldview of its author.

2.4. Eclecticism

It is difficult to locate Kindī within a specific philosophical tradition. As has been already noted by Ivry (1974, 11–21), despite an "ambivalent usage" of what might look very close to a Neoplatonic terminology, *FPh* does not develop into a Neoplatonic structure. From Neoplatonism Kindī borrows a henology consistent with the Muslim *tawḥīd*, but ignores the theory of hypostasis as well as the emanationist system (Hasnawi 1992, 655). The necessary existence of an absolute transcendent true One that provides existence to all beings while dispensing unity to them will lead to a negative theology close to the Muʿtazilī notion of *tawḥīd* as well as to the doctrine of the One proper to the *Plotiniana Arabica*. If one can find in *FPh* echoes of the *Theology of Aristotle* (see Endress 1973; D'Ancona 1998), these remain nevertheless tenuous, as noted by Hasnawi (1992, 655) compared to the more significant dependence on the Arabic fragments of Proclus's *Elements of Theology* (Endress 1973, esp. 242–46) as well as the *Platonic Theology* (Jolivet 1979), though we do not know of any Arabic translation of the latter. The influence of John Philoponus on Kindī's arguments against the eternity of the world has also been highlighted (Walzer 1962, 190–96; Davidson 1969, 370–73; Davidson 1987, 106–16), though the structure of the argumentation is different (Hasnawi 1992, 655).

Conversely *FPh* unfolds within a clearly Aristotelian framework from which it departs progressively, while it continues to operate with some of its main concepts, for example, the categories and the predicables, but also the concepts of causality, time, body, and motion. Ivry (1974, 16–18) has shown the influence of Aristotle's *Metaphysics* I and II on the opening remarks of *FPh*. Aristotle's physics looms large also, and al-Kindī borrows from the *De Caelo* even more than the *Physics*, in order to reach often non-Aristotelian conclusions.

Drawing from Aristotle, the Neoplatonic tradition as well as the Greek commentators, *FPh* elaborates a complex and original synthesis that culminates with a demonstration of the absolute unity of the first Cause where the philosophical discourse ultimately yields to a theological development that concludes with the identity of the Neoplatonic true One with the Creator and One God of Islam.

2.5. Mathematical Method

In several of his extant philosophical treatises, including not only *FPh* but also *On the Quiddity of What Cannot Be Infinite and What Is Called Infinite* (*Quiddity* hereafter), and his *Epistle to Muḥammad b. al-Jahm on the Oneness of God and the Finiteness of the Body of the Universe* (*Oneness* hereafter), as well as the one to Muḥammad al-Khurasānī *Explaining the Finiteness of the Body of the Universe* (*Finiteness* hereafter), Kindī uses a geometrical method of argumentation clearly inspired by Euclid's *Elements*. As a matter of fact, the reader of *FPh* cannot but be struck by the extensive usage of the axiomatic method, for example in chapter 2, and the proof by reductio ad absurdum that looms large in Kindī's method of argumentation throughout the whole treatise. The above-mentioned treatises are all concerned by proving the finiteness of the universe, and, in one way or another, each one of them deals with one of the issues addressed in the second chapter of *FPh*. In all of them Kindī follows, more or less, the same Euclidian pattern of argumentation: providing first definitions of the main terms, then listing the "first true and immediately intelligible premises" (*Rasāʾil* 1:114.12; *Œuvres* 29.8), in other words the axioms, and finally proceeding to the proof by deduction often following an argument by reductio ad absurdum (Rashed 2008, 132).

Al-Kindī was himself a scientist and a mathematician who, according to Nadīm's *Fihrist*, devoted at least sixty treatises to mathematics in its four branches (*Fihrist*, 256–58; Rashed 1993, 7), among them several commentaries on Euclid's *Elements*. However, what is at stake here is the application of the geometrical method to the philosophical inquiry, despite the fact that some of the treatises mentioned above are listed by Nadīm, under the "books on astronomy" (*kutub al-falakiyyāt*). This being said, Kindī wrote also a treatise titled *That Philosophy Can Only Be Acquired through the Mathematical Science* (*Fī annahu lā tunālu al-falsafa illā bi-ʿilm al-riyāḍiyyāt*, see *Fihrist*, 255), which is no longer extant.

At any rate, it is worth noting that in the second chapter of *FPh*, he establishes explicitly the mathematical examination (*al-faḥṣ al-taʿlīmī/al-faḥṣ al-riyāḍī*) as the most appropriate method of investigation for "what has no matter" (*Œuvres* 23.20,23; *Rasāʾil* 1:111.1,4), that is, metaphysics. Al-Kindī's philosophy is "written in geometrical terms" (Jolivet 2004, 679) paradoxically in order to reach, through sound but industrious geometrical proofs, the truths of the "divine science" (*al-ʿilm al-ilāhī*) immediately accessible to the prophets (for further details on the place of mathematics in al-Kindī's classification of theoretical sciences, see Endress 2003, 129-130; Gutas 2004; Adamson 2007a, 30-37; Gannagé, forthcoming).

2.6. Creation of a Philosophical Terminology

The program Kindī draws at the beginning of *FPh* leaves little doubt as to his awareness of being the first philosopher to write in Arabic. The foremost philosophers he invokes as his forerunners did not share his language (*al-mubarrizīn min al-mutafalsifīn qablana, min ghayr ahl lisāninā, Œuvres* 11.21; *Rasāʾil* 1:102.5), as he is careful to point out. That places him as the direct heir to a Greek philosophical tradition and puts on his shoulders a burden he outlines in the introduction of *FPh* (*Œuvres* 13.19–22; *Rasāʾil* 1:103.8–11): that is, to present what the ancients have dealt with completely and to complete what they left unfinished, "*following, in so doing, the custom of the language* and the usages of the time."

Language is at the heart of Kindī's enterprise of transmission of Greek philosophy and sciences into Arabic, as he himself emphasizes by constantly referring to his own community, in that context, as "the people speaking our language" (*ahl lisāninā*) (Rosenthal 1956, 445 n. 2). Gerhard Endress has shown that Kindī was the patron and the *spiritus rector* of a circle of translators recognizable by a distinctive phraseology and terminology—they would also share with Kindī's own writings—characterized, for example, by the use of loanwords or direct transliterations from Greek, the formation of neologisms, and an often rough style reflecting Greek stylistic constructions (Endress 1973, 75–155; Endress 1997, 58–62).

FPh is emblematic of such a philosophical terminology, which was still in the making at that early stage of the transmission of Greek philosophy into Arabic. It is fraught with neologisms intended to render abstract universals or philosophical concepts for which no Arabic term had yet been coined. Among the most representative examples are terms gravitating around the concept of being, like *inniyya* or *anniyya*. Most probably derived from the Arabic particle *inna* or *anna* and substantified with the addition of the suffix *-iyya* in order to denote an abstract notion (Endress 1973, 77 ff.; Ivry 1974, 120–21; Adamson 2002, 299–300), it is used mostly with the meaning of existence in the affirmative sense of the existence of a particular thing but can also refer to being in general as well as to essence. Likewise, *inniyyāt* or *anniyyāt* refer most often to "the things that exist," hence echoing the Greek τὰ ὄντα.

Inniyya seems to be the equivalent of *huwiyya*, and they are often used interchangeably (e.g., *Œuvres*, 35.14–15 and 37.7–8; *Rasāʾil* 1:119.16 and 120.17–18), though the latter, being derived from the pronoun *huwa*, has sometimes the sense of being an entity, an ipseity (Ivry 1974, 159). More unusual is *tahawwī* or *taʾyīs* for bringing into existence (e.g., *Œuvres*, 41, 5; 97, 8–9; *Rasāʾil* 1:123.3, 162.1). The latter is derived from *ays*, attested in the earliest Arabic dictionary compiled by al-Khalīl (d. ca. 175/791)[2] as referring also to particular

[2] See al-Khalīl b. Aḥmad, *Kitāb al-ʿAyn*, ed. M. al-Makhzūmī and I. al-Samarrāʾī, 8 vols. (Baghdad: Dār wa-maktabat al-Hilāl), 7:300, 301. Reference kindly provided to me by Abdallah Soufan.

existence, but which, like *inniyya* and *huwiyya*, can signify being in general, especially in opposition to *lays* used as a substantive meaning nonbeing, particularly in chapter 3.

2.7. Prologue

The treatise opens with a prologue following a clear structure. It is first a praise and a defense of philosophy justifying its practice as subordinated to the study of the "science of the first Cause," considered as the noblest part of philosophy. It also lays the main points that will be developed throughout the treatise. Finally it includes a program and exposes a method: the philosopher has to build on the results of the ancient philosophers, who have paved the way in our research of the truth, and to pursue in the same way in order to further expand on them.

2.7.1. What Is First Philosophy?

Following the dedication to the caliph al-Muʿtaṣim bi-llāh, the first chapter opens with a definition of "the art of philosophy" as being the "highest human art" and the noblest in rank "whose definition is the science of the things in their true natures insofar as man is capable of that" (*Œuvres*, 9. 8–14; *Rasāʾil* 1: 97.4–98.2):

> The aim of the philosopher is to reach truth (*iṣābat al-ḥaqq*) in his science and to act according to the truth in his praxis. It is not an endless activity, for when we reach the truth, we stop and the activity ceases. We don't find what we are seeking from the truth without finding a cause. The cause of the being (*wujūd*) and stability (*thabāt*) of everything is the truth, for everything that has an existence (*inniyya*) has a truth (*ḥaqīqa*), *therefore the truth exists (mawjūd) necessarily since the existents exist (idh al-inniyāt mawjūda)*. The noblest philosophy and the highest in rank is the first philosophy, I mean the science of the first True who is the cause of every truth.[3]

As has been already observed, Kindī seems to follow here an eclectic approach (Ivry 1972, 124; *Œuvres* 101 n. 1): while borrowing mainly from Aristotle's *Metaphysics* I and

[3] The sentence in italics involves a reading that contrasts with most of the editions and translations of *FPh* (see, e.g., *Œuvres* 9.13; *Rasāʾil* 1:99.9–10 [*fa-l-ḥaqqu iḍṭirrāran mawjūdun idhan li-inniyyāt mawjūdatin*]; Ivry 1974, 55.16; and Adamson and Pormann 2012, §2), that tend to favor a Neoplatonic understanding of that passage, where the existence of beings is seen as derived from the necessary existence of the true One, though it is worth noting that the expression "the true One" does not appear in this definition. Our reading, which does not entail any amendment to the manuscript wording, is in line with Ibn Hazm's reading (see *Rasāʾil* 2:26.3 and Ibn Ḥazm, *Radd*, 189.6). It restores the inductive nature of the argument, which moves from the empirical existence of beings to the existence of a cause to such beings. Such a method of argumentation pervades much of the treatise and is characteristic of al-Kindī's style, as is the call to sensible evidence that comes up every now and then in the course of an argument.

II (esp. *Metaph.* II.1, 993b19–20), the overall definition seems also to be inspired by the prologues of the Alexandrian commentaries to Porphyre's *Isagoge* that used to start with "preliminary explanations on what is philosophy in general," including an enumeration of six different definitions of philosophy (Hadot 1989, 23), a division of philosophy between theory and practice (Hein 1985, 86 ff.), as well as an enumeration of the four Aristotelian causes (matter, form, efficient, and final) combined with the four epistemological questions, "whether," "what," "which," and "why" that we find also reproduced by Kindī few lines below (*Œuvres* 11.5; *Rasāʾil* 1:101.5) (Altmann and Stern 2009, 13 ff.). Actually, in his *Epistle on the Definitions and the Descriptions of Things*[4] (*Definitions* hereafter), Kindī provides a series of six definitions of philosophy, avowedly inspired by the Neoplatonic commentators (*al-falsafa, ḥaddahā al-qudamāʾ bi-ʿiddat ḥurūf*) without, however, corresponding exactly to the list they used to produce. The definition of *FPh* comes close to the fourth definition that considers philosophy "from the point of view of its pre-eminence" as being "the art of arts and the science of sciences" (*Rasāʾil* 1:172–73; Altmann and Stern 2009, 28–30; Ivry 1974, 125) as well as to the last one that characterizes philosophy as "the knowledge of the eternal, universal things, of their existences (*inniyyātuhā*), their quiddities (*māʾiyyātuhā*), and their causes, *according to man's capacity*," as has been already noted (*Cinq Epîtres* 1976, 58). Worth noting is that the same division between theoretical and practical philosophy occurs, in similar terms, in the prologue of *On the Great Art* (*Fī l-Ṣināʿa l-ʿuẓmā*), where it is clearly inspired by Ptolemy's preface to his *Almagest* (for further developments on that issue and the relationship between *FPh* and *On the Great Art* see Gannagé forthcoming).

At any rate, al-Kindī's main source of inspiration, here, remains Aristotle's description of philosophy in *Metaph.* II.1, 993b20 as "a knowledge of truth" that he reads in Asṭāth's translation as *ʿilm al-ḥaqq* and understands as the knowledge of the ultimate nature of things and the first principles of beings. Worth noting that *Ḥaqq* and *Awwal* are among the names of God, which allows Kindī to identify first philosophy and theology as the "science of the first Truth which is the cause of all truth," being "the cause of the existence and stability (or permanence, *thabāt*) of all things," hence reconciling the religious belief in a supreme Truth with the Aristotelian doctrine of knowledge as search for cause (D'Ancona 1998, 849).

First philosophy defined as the "science of the first Truth" will thus be further specified as "the science of the first Cause" (echoing *Metaph.* VI.1, 1026a18–23 as mentioned by Ivry 1974, 121) "given that all the content of philosophy is subsumed (*munṭawin*) in the science of the first Cause," which is thus first in nobility, first in genus, first from the point of view of what is scientifically the most certain, but also first in time "since the first Cause is the cause of time" (D'Ancona 1998, 853, maintains that next to *Metaph.* II.1, 996b10–14, this passage echoes both the preface of the *Theology of Aristotle* as well as the text itself, reproducing "the late Neoplatonic pattern of the inclusion of all the theoretical sciences within metaphysics"). Causality in time is a further hint toward a theory of creation and

[4] On the complex textual transmission of this treatise, which has been edited more than once, see Adamson 2007a, 40 and references *ad in.*

the refutation of the eternity of the world that is the object of the next chapter. Such a definition concludes the first part of the prologue, justifying the title of the whole treatise and giving it its overall orientation.

2.7.2. Assimilation of Greek Philosophy

Next, Kindī exposes the program and method we have recalled above and which he has reiterated in several of his scientific books (see, e.g., the first lines of his *De aspectibus* in Rashed 1997, 438): to build on the results of the Greeks and pursue them in the same way in order to further expand on them. The same program, in almost the same terms, closes the prologue of *On the Great Art* (Kindī, *Ṣināʿa*, 129.8–130.2). Actually, Kindī draws up a cumulative history of knowledge that seems to be freely inspired by *Metaph.* II.1, 993a30–b4 and 993b12–14: we should be grateful to all those who contributed before us to the truth, even if little, since by the union of all a significant amount has been collected. Those have been our "forerunners and our associates" because they shared with us the product of their thoughts.

> Had they not existed we would not have been able to collect, even if we were to inquire about them fervently throughout our lives, these *true principles* (*al-awāʾil al-ḥaqiyya*) through which we are able to reach the *hidden ends* (*al-awākhir al-khafiyya*) of our inquiries. This [knowledge] has been collected only in preceding eras that elapsed era after era, until our present time. (*Œuvres*, 13.2–8; *Rasāʾil* 1:102.10–16)

This being said, the time factor adds to the cumulative history of knowledge the idea of a scientific progress toward an end that is absent from Aristotle (Jolivet 1993, 74). It is actually clearly inspired by Ptolemy's *Almagest*, where the notion of the scientific progress through the additional time available is expressed not only in the preface, but also in the epilogue and throughout the book (Toomer 1984, 37 and n. 11).

2.7.3. Defense of Philosophy

The apology for Greek philosophy staked out as a foundational moment in a history of scientific progress toward the truth is not incompatible with the revelation brought by the prophets. On the contrary, both share the same content as Kindī states few lines below (*Œuvres*, 15. 9–12; *Rasāʾil* 1:104.8–10):

> The knowledge of things in their true nature includes the knowledge of sovereignty (*ʿilm al-rubūbiyya*), the knowledge of oneness (*ʿilm al-waḥdāniyya*), the knowledge of excellence, and on the whole the knowledge of everything beneficial and of the way to it, while staying away from all harm and protecting oneself against it. Acquiring all these, this is what the truthful apostles brought from God, great be His praise.

The profession of such a harmony (*al-qawl ʿalā l-rubūbiyya* is also the title born by the *Theology of Aristotle*, as noted by Jolivet, see *Œuvres*, 15 n. 13 and references therein) is accompanied by a long and violent invective against unidentified opponents who "oppose the acquisition of knowledge of the things in their true nature and call it unbelief." They are contemporaries of Kindī "who have claimed speculation for themselves" (*al-muttasimūn bi-l-naẓar fī dahrinā*) and who seem to occupy high positions of power. For want of identifying these people, on whose identity there is so far no scholarly consensus, we can at least point to some elements that may help narrowing down the scope of the discussion:

The treatise is dedicated to the caliph al-Muʿtaṣim whose patronage Kindī used to benefit from, knowing that he was appointed as a tutor to his son Aḥmad. At that time he was thus in favor at the court.

The people against whom he launches his invective seem also to be in positions of power and authority as he himself underlines by describing them as occupying "fraudulent seats they have set up undeservedly." This is confirmed by Ibn Ḥazm, who identifies them as "*ahl al-riʾāsa*," when introducing an extensive part of this passage he quotes, among other extracts of *FPh*, in his refutation of Kindī's characterization of God as a cause (Ibn Ḥazm, *Radd*, 189.17).

Moreover, not only do they claim to deal with speculation (*al-muttasimūn bi-l-naẓar*), they also seem to use their positions of power in order to achieve authority in matters of religion with which they traffic (*li-al-taraʾʾus wa-l-tijāra bi-l-dīn*).

All these elements seem to point toward a group of theologians close to the sphere of power—who, at that time, must have been Muʿtazilites of some sort—as the accusation of "dirty envy," raised by Kindī, seems to hint, within the context of the fierce competition that was prevailing at the caliph's court. Given the extreme diversity of people and doctrines that characterized this early period of the movement of *iʿtizāl*, any attempt to try to identify them more precisely becomes uncertain and in any case exceeds the scope of this chapter. This being said, it seems worth noting that what is at stake here seems to be the creed of the absolute oneness of God rather than the opposition to the "philosophical inheritance of the Greeks" (see Adamson 2007a, 22–25 for the latter view). Twice during his diatribe, Kindī states, in defense of philosophy, that "the knowledge of things in their true nature" includes the knowledge of sovereignty as well as the knowledge of oneness (of God) (*Œuvres*, 15, 9, and 23). The closing lines of his tirade describe quite eloquently the object of *FPh* as "establishing the proof of the sovereignty [of God] and making evident His oneness, chasing away those who oppose Him (*al-muʿānidūn lahu*) and do not believe in Him." *FPh* seems thus a philosophical contribution to the theological discussions of the time over the concept of *tawḥīd* (for the application of the philosophical method to the treatment of theological problems see Adamson 2003). In that respect two elements are worth recalling: (1) *FPh* has passed to posterity mainly under the name of *Kitāb fī l-Tawḥīd*, as shown at the beginning of this chapter, even though al-Kindī refers to it always as *On First Philosophy*; (2) the two works that have preserved for us fragments of *FPh* have done so in relation to the issue of *tawḥīd*: directly for Ibn Ḥazm, who reproaches Kindī for having been inconsistent when describing God as a cause, which implies immediately an effect and hence precludes His oneness, while at the same time denying any multiplicity in God; indirectly for Ibn ʿAbd Rabbih, who addresses the issue of God's will, hence alluding to the controversy between Ashʿarites and Muʿtazilites concerning the definition of whether God's will is an attribute of essence or of action (see *Œuvres*, 129–30 and n. 7). Even though both of them might reflect theological and philosophical issues that were shaped after the time of Kindī, they nevertheless build on *FPh* as related in a way or another to such issues.

2.8. Proving That the World Is Finite (Chapter 2)

The first chapter had concluded with the existence of the first Truth as a first Cause that is not only the cause of every truth and "of the existence and permanence of every thing" but also "the Cause of time." That entails proving the finiteness of the sensible world and hence the finiteness of body, time, and motion. The second chapter[5] thus starts with a series of preliminary methodological "admonitions" (*waṣāya*) that aim to demonstrate that "the science of what is above the natural things is the science of what does not move" (*Œuvres*, 25.9–10; *Rasāʾil* 1:111.13). It thus requires an intellectual perception only, and therefore only the mathematical method applies to it. The first part of the chapter, to which Kindī refers as an "introduction" (*muqaddima*) (*Œuvres*, 23.10; *Rasāʾil* 1:110.10), sets thus the epistemological cadre through which one has to understand the arguments against the eternity of the world that are treated in the second part.

Kindī starts by distinguishing two types of perceptions: "one closer to us and farther with respect to nature and this is the sensory perception (*wujūd al-ḥawāss*)" (*Œuvres*, 19.4–5; *Rasāʾil* 1:106.4), which is unstable due to the changing nature of its object "as it always applies to body"; and the other "more familiar to nature and farther from us, and it is the intellectual perception (*wujūd al-ʿaql*)," which is "certain through the veracity of the intellectual principles that are necessarily intelligible, like 'it is and it is not are not true of one and the same thing' is immutable" (*Œuvres*, 19.24–21.2; *Rasāʾil* 1:107.12–13). This first example that illustrates the principle of noncontradiction (Ivry 1974, 137) is followed by another more complex one: "Outside the body of the universe, there is neither void nor plenum (*lā khalāʾ wa-lā malāʾ*), meaning neither vacuity (*farāgh*) nor body." "Neither void nor plenum . . . is a thing perceived only and necessarily by the intellect through these premises that we set forth" (*Œuvres* 21.15–18; *Rasāʾil* 1:109.1–5). The argument

[5] For a discussion of the whole or parts of this chapter see Davidson 1969, 370–373; Davidson 1987, 106–16; Craig 1979; Jolivet 1993; and Adamson 2007a, chap. 4.

then unfolds in two steps in order to show, first, the impossibility of the existence of an absolute void and, second, the impossibility that there exists a plenum beyond the body of the universe. "This follows necessarily and is not represented in the soul, but it is only a necessary intellectual perception (*wujūd ʿaqlī iḍṭirārī*)" (*Œuvres* 23.6–7; *Rasāʾil* 1:110.5–7).

Kindī endorses here a thesis defended by Aristotle not exactly in the *Physics* (IV 6–9), where only the question of the impossibility of the void is raised, but rather in the *De Caelo* (278b 21ff. and 279a 5 ff.) where he finds the issue of the denial of any void outside the "extreme circumference" addressed within the demonstration denying the existence of any body and hence any plenum outside the heaven. However, Kindī does not seem here much interested in the empirical argument against the possibility of void outside the extreme limit of the universe, as noted by Ivry. He seems to be "rather thinking of the void in some absolute logical sense which allows him to establish an immediate self-contradiction of terms" (Ivry 1974, 139).

In fact, the bulk of the argument is devoted to the refutation of the possibility of a plenum outside the universe, which constitutes a step further toward his demonstration of the noneternity of the world. In order to prove that the sensible world is finite, Kindī needed to rule out, at least logically, the possibility of any plenum outside the physical world. He still had to prove that there can be no actual infinity—as he himself admits (*Œuvres* 21.25–22.1; *Rasāʾil* 1:109.14)—in order to show that the world is a finite magnitude and thus eternity applies only to the first One.

The three arguments against the eternity of the world that follow are also preceded by a series of "rules" (*qawānīn*) that need to be observed in that art, and these consist of a series of definitions concerning the nature of the eternal. They are followed by three short arguments intended to prove through a reductio ad absurdum that the eternal has no genus, nor does it undergo any corruption, alteration, or change whatsoever, and hence, "The eternal is necessarily perfect" (*fa-l-azalī tāmmun iḍṭirāran*):

> The eternal is that which does absolutely not necessitate "it is not" (*inna l-azalī huwa alladhī lam yajib "laysa huwa" muṭlaqan*); hence, as far as generation is concerned, the eternal has no "before" to its existence (*li-hawiyyatihi*); the eternal is that whose subsistence is not through something else; the eternal has no cause (*ʿilla*); the eternal has no substrate and no predicate, no agent and no reason (*sabab*)—I mean that for the sake of which it would exist, for there are no causes other than the ones previously mentioned. (*Œuvres* 27.8–11; *Rasāʾil* 1:113.1–4)

The "causes previously mentioned" are the four Aristotelian causes mentioned in chapter 1, and Kindī is thus ruling out in these premises the possibility of any physical treatment of the eternal in what follows. Having no cause, the eternal is thus naturally incompatible with any kind of change. As has been already observed (Ivry 1974, 142–43; Adamson 2007a, 98), Kindī is anticipating here the arguments of sections 3 and 4, and the "eternal" that is immutable is God. Indeed, God alone is perfect. The argument concludes from the incompatibility of eternity and change to the incompatibility of eternity and body: "Since body has a genus and species and what is eternal has no genus, the body is not the eternal (*fa-l-jirm <ghayr> al-azalī*)" (*Œuvres* 29.5; *Rasāʾil* 1:114.8–9). The three following arguments focus on proving that the world, being a body, has a beginning and an end.

2.8.1. Three Arguments against the Infinity of the World

The following arguments are also reproduced in one way or another, partially or in full, in three other short treatises Kindī devoted to the issue of the eternity of the world. *Quiddity* (*Rasāʾil* 1:193–98; *Œuvres* 149–55) reproduces with slight differences the first argument, which proves that time and body cannot be infinite, in order to show that there is no infinite in actuality. As for *Oneness* (*Rasāʾil* 1:199–207; *Œuvres* 135–47), it replicates almost verbatim important passages from *FPh* (see the introduction and the notes in *Œuvres* 149–55), to which it adds a proof of the existence of God and its oneness that is missing in *FPh*. Finally, *Finiteness* (*Rasāʾil* 1:185–92; *Œuvres* 158–65) offers mathematical demonstrations of some of the principles used in *FPh* as axioms. The issue of the eternity *a parte post* that is addressed in *FPh* is missing from the three of them (*Œuvres* 149).

2.8.1.1. *Body, Movement, and Time Do Not Precede Each Other*

The first argument against the eternity of the world in *FPh* aims at proving that body, time, and movement do not precede each other and hence, if time is finite, "the extension of the existence" of the universe is finite (Hasnawi 1992, 655). It relies on the assumption that time is not a being (*al-zamān laysa bi-mawjūd*, *Œuvres* 31, 23) but is an attribute of the body (*maḥmūl*) like magnitude, place, and movement (Jolivet 1993, 56). Kindī starts by proving the impossibility of an infinite magnitude:

> Let us say now that no body, nor anything else that has quantity and quality, can be infinite in actuality (*lā nihāya lahu bi-l-fiʿl*) and that infinity (*lā nihāya*) is only in potentiality. (*Œuvres* 29.6–7; *Rasāʾil* 1:114.10–11)

The argument then unfolds in four steps. Following a Euclidian form, it starts (*a*) with a series of six axioms or "first true immediately intelligible premises" (*muqaddimāt uwwal ḥaqqiyya maʿqūla bi-lā-tawassuṭ*), four of which Kindī will use in his subsequent argumentation (nos. 2, 3, 5, and 6; cf. Craig 1979, 27), like "[bodies] with an equal distance between their limits are equal in actuality and potentiality" (axiom 2) or "what has a limit is not infinite" (axiom 3) (*Œuvres* 29.10–11; *Rasāʾil* 1:114.13–14). Given these premises, and applying throughout the whole argument the method of reductio ad absurdum, al-Kindī ends up proving (*b*) that no magnitude can be infinite in actuality by showing the absurdities that will loom when one tries to apply ordinary arithmetic operations to magnitudes hypothetically infinite (Hasnawi 1992, 655). Having thus shown "that it is impossible for a body to be infinite" and therefore that no magnitude can be infinite in actuality, Kindī moves to (*c*) the third step of the argument:

> Since time is a quantity, it is impossible that there be an infinite time in actuality, considering that time has a finite beginning. Also, things attributed to a finite [body] are necessarily finite; therefore every attribute of a body, be it magnitude, place, movement, or time—which is divided (*mufaṣṣal*) by motion—and the sum total of all the attributes of the body in actuality, is also finite, since body is finite; hence the body of the universe is finite, as is every one of its attributes. (*Œuvres* 31.10–14; *Rasāʾil* 1:116.7–12)

The finiteness of time appears to be either a direct consequence of the proof of the finiteness of any magnitude, time itself being a magnitude, or an indirect consequence of the finiteness in extension of the universe, time being then finite as an attribute of the universe (Hasnawi 1992, 655). Hence, from the impossibility of the existence of any infinite magnitude in actuality al-Kindī concludes:

> Since this is necessary, it has been made clear that an infinite time in actuality cannot exist. Now time is the time of the body of the universe, I mean its extension (*muddatuhu*). If time is finite, the existence of the body is finite, since time is not an existent and there is no body without time, because time is the number of movement—I mean it is an extension measured by movement (*mudda taʿudduhā l-ḥaraka*). Therefore, if there is a movement, there is time, and if there is no movement, there is no time. (*Œuvres* 31.21–25; *Rasāʾil* 1:117.1–6)

In the background looms the famous Aristotelian formula of *Phys.* IV 12, 220b 14–16 and, as already noted by Jolivet (Jolivet 1993, 56–58), all the concepts at stake (time being a magnitude; time and movement being defined by each other; time being the number of the movement of the sphere of the fixed stars) are drawn from *Phys.* IV 10–14.

Having shown that body, time, and motion are coextensive and finite, Kindī still has to rule out a possibility (*d*): what if someone "thought that it is possible for the body of the universe (*jirm al-kull*) to have been at rest first, having the potentiality to move, and then to have moved?" In other words Kindī still had to examine whether a universe, which is assumed to have been originally at rest and then to have moved, can be said to be generated from nothing or be eternal (cf. *Phys.* VIII 1, esp. 250b 24, where the view of the body of the universe being first at rest was attributed by Aristotle to Anaxagoras though, as noted by Ivry 1974, 157–58, the two texts have different orientations). Having shown that movement is finite, Kindī still has to preclude the possibility of an infinite rest, which he does on the assumption that generation, understood here as the coming into existence out of nothing (*fa-in kāna kawnan ʿan lays fa-inna tahawwīhi aysan ʿan laysa*), "is one of the species of motion." Since body cannot have preceded its generation, then generation "is its essence," and hence the being of the body is not prior to movement. On the other hand if the universe was eternally at rest, motion could never arise, for motion is change and the eternal does not change, it simply is. Therefore it is self-contradictory to say that the universe is eternal and yet motion has a beginning. Kindī can now conclude:

> Thus, if there is movement, there is necessarily body, and if there is body, there is necessarily movement. But we already said that time does not precede movement;

> thus necessarily time does not precede body, since there is no time but with movement, and since there is no body but with movement and there is no movement but with a body, and no body without extension (*mudda*), given that extension is that in which there is existence (*huwiyya*), I mean that in which there is a certain existent (*huwa mā*). . . . Thus body, movement, and time do not precede each other. . . . Body does not precede time; thus it is impossible for the body of the universe (*jirm al-kull*) to be infinite as far as its existence (*inniyyatihi*) is concerned. The existence of the body of the universe is necessarily finite and hence it is impossible for the body of the universe to be eternal. (*Œuvres* 35.11–22; *Rasāʾil* 1:119.12–120.5)

Beyond the coextensivity of body, movement, and time, whose background might be *Phys.* IV 11, 219a 10–18 (see also *Quiddity, Œuvres*153.12–24; *Rasāʾil* 1:196.3–197.3 for the same argument in abbreviated form), the concept of extension looms large (Jolivet 1993, 57 and 62 ff.). Closely associated with *anniyya* and *huwiyya*, of which it is the correlate, *mudda* is the receptacle of anything that exists in the world and hence the sign of the finiteness of any existence here below. Being common to time and body, its centrality will be crucial for the demonstration of the spatial as well as temporal finiteness of the world, as will be confirmed in the next argument.

2.8.1.2. *Proof by Composition*

This proof, intended to show the finiteness of body, is based on the double composition of bodies, every body being composed (*murakkab*) of matter and form or substance and tridimensionality. But composition is a change (*tabaddul*) (affecting the state of noncomposition) and thus it is a movement. Without movement there is no body since body is composite. Hence body and motion do not precede each other but are coexistent.

Time and movement are likewise coexistent, because movement is a change and the change is "the number of the extension of what changes" (*al-tabaddul ʿadad muddat al-mutabaddil*). And time is an extension numbered by movement. Every body has an extension, meaning "that in which there is existence (*mā huwa fīhi inniyya*), I mean that in which there is a certain existent (*huwa mā*)" (*Œuvres* 37.8; *Rasāʾil* 1:120.17–18). But body does not precede movement, nor the extension numbered by movement, and hence body, movement, and time "are together as far as existence is concerned" (*fa-hiya maʿan fī l-anniyya*). As a result, time is finite in actuality since the existence of body is finite in actuality.

The whole argument rests on the assumption that composition is to be understood as a kind of change and hence a species of movement (*in kāna l-tarkīb wa-l-taʾlīf tabaddulan mā*) (for further developments see Davidson 1987, 111–13). This is even more clearly stated in *Oneness* (*Œuvres* 143.4; *Rasāʾil* 1:204.16: "Among the sorts of change (*tabaddul*) there are composition and assembling because it is the arrangement of things and their combination").

The proof of the finiteness of bodies as well as its corollary, the finiteness of time as an accident of body, are both intended to show the dependence of any created existence on the true and eternal One whose oneness and eternity is radically exclusive of any plurality and extension (Jolivet 1993, 64 n. 28).

While the second argument remains along the lines of the first one, aiming at reinforcing it in order "to increase, for those who examine that method, their expertise in engaging in it" (*Œuvres* 35. 23–24; *Rasāʾil* 1:120.5–6), Kindī tells us that the third and final argument against the infinity of the world is "of another sort": "Let us now make clear with another sort [of argument] (*nawʿ*) that time cannot be infinite in actuality neither in its past nor in its future" (*Œuvres* 37.14–15; *Rasāʾil* 1:121.3–4).

2.8.1.3a. *Argument for the Finiteness of Past Time*

The argument unfolds in two steps: (*a*) from the impossibility of an infinite series of past segments of time Kindī draws (*b*) the impossibility of traversing a temporal infinity in order to reach a given time and thus concludes that the present could never have been reached if an infinite past were to precede it. In other words, the present could never have been reached if infinite past time or an infinite series of past segments of time had to be traversed (Jolivet 1993, 64–65). But we reach a definite time (*al-intihāʾ ilā zaman maḥdūd mawjūd*); hence time does not proceed (*muqbilan*) from infinity but necessarily from a limit. The extension of the body is thus not infinite, and it is impossible that a body exists without extension. Therefore the existence of a body (*inniyyat al-jirm*) is not infinite, but the existence of a body is finite. Thus it is impossible for a body to be eternal. This argument, based on the impossibility to traverse the infinite, is also used by the Muʿtazilite theologian al-Naẓẓām (Wolfson 1976, 416–17; Davidson 1969, 375–76; Davidson 1987, 125).

2.8.1.3b. *Impossibility of an Infinite Series of Future Segments of Time*

Finally, after proving that past time cannot be infinite, Kindī had to complete the last step of his argument and prove that future time is not infinite either (*FPh* is the only one of the four treatises Kindī has devoted to the eternity of the world that addresses the question of the eternity *a parte post*). No matter what "definite time" might be added to the already accumulated finite past time, the total sum will remain finite.

The three arguments, intended to prove the finiteness of the world, entail de facto its creation or at least its beginning and hence the necessity of a first cause. Kindī had already established in the prologue the existence of a first Cause described as "the cause of time" (*ʿillat al-zamān*). However, he still needs to go through a long detour (chaps. 3 and 4) in order to establish that the "first true One" is the cause of the unity and the existence (*ʿillat al-tahawwī*) of all things, being one by essence, whereas "what is being brought into existence (*yuhawwā*) is not eternal."

Having thus proven that body, time, and motion are finite and having stated that "the body of the universe is a being coming to be from nonbeing" (*jirm al-kull kawn ʿan lays*) (*Œuvres* 33.24; *Rasāʾil* 1:119.4) whose "existence is necessarily finite" (*Œuvres* 35.22; *Rasāʾil* 1:120.3), Kindī needs now to rule out the possibility of anything, here below, being the cause of its own essence before addressing the issue of the unmoved cause of movement, as he has announced at the beginning of the second chapter (*Œuvres* 25.6–9; *Rasāʾil* 1:111.10–13):

> What is above natural [things] (*al-ṭabīʿiyyāt*) does not move, because it is impossible for a thing to be the cause of the coming to be of its essence, as we will show shortly. Hence, the cause of movement is not a movement, nor does the cause of what moves move: thus what is above natural things does not move.

2.9. Unity in the Sensible World (Chapter 3)

2.9.1. A Thing Cannot Be the Cause of Itself

The third chapter of *FPh* opens with the following inquiry, to which the first section is devoted: "Is it possible for a thing to be the cause of the coming-to-be of its essence (*ʿillat kawn dhātihi*), or is that impossible?" (*Œuvres* 41, 3–5) Kindī proceeds to explain immediately that he is using *kawn* in a specific and unusual sense, since his inquiry will include the possibility of a generation ex nihilo while generation is usually said to be out of something else:

> I mean by the coming-to-be (*kawn*) of its essence, its being brought into existence (*tahawwīhi*) out of something *or out of nothing*. Indeed—in other places—coming-to-be is said particularly of what comes-to-be *out of something*, because it is necessary for the thing either to be a being (*aysun*) and its essence a nonbeing (*laysun*), or to be a nonbeing and its essence a being; or to be a nonbeing and its essence a nonbeing; or to be a being and its essence a being. (*Œuvres* 41.5–8; *Rasāʾil* 1:123.3–6)

With this question he is paving the way not only for the conclusion of the chapter that will establish the necessity of a first Cause, which in turn will be the cause of the coming-to-be and the permanence of everything, but also for the last lines of the treatise that will infer from the noneternity of anything being-brought-into-existence (*yuhawwā*), its creation and hence the necessity of a creator.

In what follows, Kindī examines in each case the possibility for a thing to be the cause of its own essence, applying a reductio ad absurdum style of argument, in order to show the contradictions to which such an assumption will lead. He then concludes that in none of the cases that he lists can a thing be said to be the cause of its essence. One of the main threads of the argument is the radical distinction between the cause and its effect, and hence the impossibility for a thing to be the cause of its essence if it were to be identical with it, since the effect cannot be identical with its cause. Kindī does not specify further the nature of the distinction between the cause and its effect, though it constitutes the backbone of his argument, as the closing sentence of the chapter shows, echoing the prologue of the treatise:

> It has been made clear that all things have a first Cause that is not of the same genus, nor of the same figure, nor similar [to them] or participating in them. Rather it is loftier, nobler, and prior to them, and it is the cause of their coming-to-be and their permanence. (*Œuvres* 67.17–19; *Rasāʾil* 1:143.1–2)

In the meantime Kindī had shown that in everything unity and multiplicity are associated due to a cause that is "neither multiple nor is it multiple and one" because

> if it is multiple, then there would be unity in it, because multiplicity is nothing other than an aggregate of units. It would thus be a multiplicity and a unity at the same time, and hence the cause of multiplicity and unity would be unity and multiplicity and the thing would be the cause of its essence. But the cause is other than the effect, and hence the thing would be other than its essence, which is absurd and impossible. Thus the first Cause is neither multiple nor is it multiple and one. It thus remains that the cause is only one, with no multiplicity together with it in any way whatsoever. (*Œuvres* 67.19–24; *Rasāʾil* 1:143.4–8)

But in order to reach that conclusion, Kindī had to show that anything that is not essential in something, that is, anything that is accidental (*ʿāriḍ*), is an effect produced by something else in which it is essential.

2.9.2. Unity Is an Effect and an Accident in All Predicables and What They Are Said Of

Hence, in the second section of the chapter, and after having defined all the concepts he needed for his subsequent argument, we see Kindī examining "in how many ways 'one' (*wāḥid*) is said" (*Œuvres* 45.16; *Rasāʾil* 1:126.14), since "one" is said "of each one of the predicables (*maqūlāt*) and what comes to be from the predicables (*al-kāʾin min al-maqūlāt*) insofar as it is a genus, a species, an individual (*shakhṣ*), a specific difference, a proper, a common accident, an all, a part, a whole, a some" (*Œuvres* 47.12–14; *Rasāʾil* 1:128.4–6).

The inquiry is carried out upon each one of the universals listed by Kindī in order to investigate how "one" is said of each one of them. In each case the conclusion is invariably the same: in each one of the universals, unity is by convention (*bi-l-waḍʿ*) since they are all said of a multiplicity of a certain sort. Unity is thus said in a nonessential way (*min jihha lā dhātiyya*) of the universals, and does not belong to any of them in truth (*al-waḥda fīhi laysat bi-ḥaqīqiyya*); it is thus accidental, meaning "it is acquired from something else" (*mustafād min ghayrihi*). In other words, "It is acquired from a dispenser (*mufīd*), and it is an affection (*athar*)." Kindī then concludes:

> Furthermore, anything that is in something else accidentally is yet in another thing essentially because anything that is in something by accident is in something else by essence. Hence, since we have shown that unity is in all these [predicables] by

> accident, then it is in something else by essence and not by accident. Hence unity—in that in which unity is acquired by accident—comes from that in which it is by essence. Therefore, there is necessarily a true One (*wāḥid ḥaqq*) whose unity is not an affection. Let us clarify that more fully than what has been mentioned above. (*Œuvres* 53.10–15; *Rasāʾil* 1:132.8–14)

The first step of the argument concludes already with the necessary existence of a true One, in which unity is essential and is not an effect. That is a true One who dispenses unity in everything else in which unity is thus by accident.

Worth noting is the opposition "by accident" versus "by essence" that, next to the opposition "cause" versus "effect", is another thread articulating the whole argument. Here it is doubled up with the pair affection/effecter[6] (*muʾaththir*), which is also found in Kindī's *On the True Agent* (*Œuvres* 167–71; *Rasāʾil* 1:180–84). The emphasis is on the nature of the unity as an acquired character and thus not part of the essence of the thing.

The concepts are still Aristotelian, but they are already catering to a henology that starts being noticed with the apparition of a "true One in which unity is not an affection," who will thus be the cause of the unity that is an accident and an effect in the created things. Gerhard Endress has shown that the idea of unity as an "affection" of things, insofar as they participate in the true unity, is inspired by the Arabic version of Proclus, *Elements of Theology*, proposition 3, according to which the participated unity is an affection of what is, in itself, multiplicity (Endress 1973, 245; D'Ancona 1995b, 160). In fact, this idea will loom large in the conclusion of chapter 4, and by the same token of the first book of *FPh*. For now, Kindī is just paving the way for it and, as shown by D'Ancona, might be rather inspired by the Arabic version of proposition 2 (D'Ancona 1995b, 185–87). At any rate, it is definitely in the second part of chapter 3 that the influence of the Arabic Proclus is most significant.

2.9.3. Unity and Multiplicity Always Coexist in the Sensible World

In the third section of the chapter, and in order to "clarify" what he had just exposed, Kindī lists a series of arguments intended to prove that we cannot find in "all that is perceived by the senses and whose quiddity is grasped by the intellect" (*Œuvres* 53.16–17; *Rasāʾil* 1:132.15–16) multiplicity without unity (nine arguments) nor unity without

[6] In order to render the intended redundancy of the Arabic pair *athar*/*muʾaththir*, I follow here Jolivet and Rashed who specify that they take the word "effecteur" in its philosophical sense attested at the end of the 18th c. as meaning "efficient" (*Œuvres*, 46 n. 46), knowing however that the Latin *effector* (person who creates or causes) has been preserved in English as meaning an "effecter" i.e. "A person who or thing which brings about an event or result, accomplishes a purpose, etc. or a "maker, a creator " (OID).

multiplicity (nine arguments). That leads him, in the fourth and concluding section of the chapter, to establish the existence of a first Cause that is only one (*wāḥida faqaṭ*), and hence radically different from the sensible things (in which unity is always mixed) and the cause of their coming-to-be and their permanence.

All the arguments follow a similar pattern starting with the hypothetical premise of a multiplicity without unity (or vice versa, assuming a unity without multiplicity) from which is deduced, through a reductio ad absurdum, a conclusion that contradicts either the premise or the factual experience. The whole passage bears a strong Proclean influence (Endress 1973, 242–43; and, more strikingly, Jolivet 1979, who has shown that this series of dialectic arguments bears strong parallels with Proclus's *Platonic Theology*, though it is unclear how Kindī could have accessed the work of which no Arabic translation is known).

The argument culminates in the fourth and final section of the chapter that concludes with the result that unity and plurality coexist necessarily in the sensible world, where one is never found without the other.

> It has thus been shown from all these inquiries that it is impossible that there is multiplicity without unity in anything that we have mentioned, and from some of [these inquiries] that it is impossible that anything at all be unity without multiplicity. It has thus been made clear that it is impossible that there is unity only (*waḥda faqaṭ*), without multiplicity or multiplicity only, without unity. . . . It remains then that unity participates in multiplicity, that is, participates in it in all sensible things, and in what attaches to sensible things. That is to say, in whichever among them there is multiplicity there is unity and in whichever there is unity there is multiplicity. (*Œuvres* 63.17–65.3; *Rasāʾil* 1:140.10–141.3)

Kindī still has to show that the interdependence of unity and multiplicity in the sensible world requires "another cause, other than their essence, loftier, more noble than them, and prior to both of them, since the cause is by essence prior to the effect" (*Œuvres* 67.1–3; *Rasāʾil* 1:142.11–13). Now this cause is either one or multiple. If it is multiple it will have also unity, and thus unity and multiplicity will become the cause of unity and multiplicity, which is absurd. "Thus the first Cause is not multiple, nor is it multiple and one. It remains then that the cause is only one, with no multiplicity together with it in no way whatsoever" (*Œuvres* 67.23–24; *Rasāʾil* 1:143.7–8. For the Neoplatonic background of this passage see Endress 1973, 243–44, who shows the parallels with the Arabic version of prop. 5 of Proclus's *Elements of Theology*).

The chapter thus ends with the appearance of a first transcendent Cause that is not yet identified with God or the Creator. Kindī still has to show "in which way unity exists in the things that are caused (*al-maʿlūlāt*), what is true unity, and what is unity metaphorically and not in truth" (*Œuvres* 69.3–5; *Rasāʾil* 1:143.10–12), hence introducing the program of the fourth and last chapter of what has reached us from *On First Philosophy*.

2.10. The True One and the One Creator (Chapter 4)

"Let us now say in which way unity exists in the predicables (*al-maqūlāt*), what is one in truth and what is one metaphorically and not in truth" (*Œuvres* 71.3–4; *Rasāʾil* 1:143.14–15). The opening sentence of chapter 4[7] echoes the closing sentence of chapter 3, in such a striking way that the reader might very well miss the slight differences between both sentences that may turn out to be more significant than it appears at first sight (see also Ivry 1974, 179): (1) *al-maʿlūlāt* (things that are caused) is replaced by *al-maqūlāt* (predicables), hence paving the way for the conclusion of the chapter where all the intelligibles (*al-maʿqūlāt*) are denied from the One. The predicables are all universals and thus intelligibles. (2) There is a terminological shift from "unity" to "one" that reflects the progression of the inquiry: while chapter 3 examined all the ways unity is in sensible things, chapter 4 tries to specify in which way "one" can apply to God and hence what is the nature of the true one, in other words what can be truly said to be One. (3) The dichotomy "one metaphorically" versus "one in truth" appears for the first time and does not overlap completely with the pair "accidentally one" versus "essentially one" as we will shortly see.

Kindī introduces in the first section a discussion in an attempt to rule out, through a series of obscure arguments, any possibility of "one" being a number and hence being a quantity to which will apply any of the predicates that apply to quantity like equal and unequal or divisibility and nondivisibility. Incidentally, and as we will see below, these pages reveal a theory of number that would be worth further investigation, though that clearly exceeds the scope of this chapter.

2.10.1. One Is Not a Number

Indeed, "Most distinctive of a quantity is its being called both equal and unequal" (*Cat.* 6, 6a 26–27). Hence, according to Kindī, one, if a number and thus a quantity, would be divisible into numerous ones, some of which are equal to it and some not (as noted by Ivry 1974, 181, al-Kindī obviously understands the statement as meaning that the one itself would have to possess equal and unequal parts). But one is indivisible by definition. There is thus an obvious contradiction and thus one is not a number (*Œuvres* 73.19–75.1; *Rasāʾil* 1:146.18–147.5). By the same token, Kindī reminds us not to confuse the one with the matter that is unified by the one, or to say it differently, not to confuse what we count with what we count with. A class of material things "is composed of numerable things not of number" (*maʿdūdāt lā ʿadad*). Thus, "When we say 'five horses,'

[7] For a discussion of this chapter see Marmura and Rist 1963 and Adamson 2007a, chap. 3.

the horses are numbered by the five, which is a number with no matter; matter is only in the horses" (*Œuvres* 75.3–5; *Rasāʾil* 1:147.8–9). In other words, Kindī seems to think of numbers as "abstractions from groups made up of pure units which are abstraction from physical objects" (see *Phys.* 219b 5–7 and Annas 1976, 34) and hence "We must not confuse the one with that which is rendered a single thing by the one" (Marmura and Rist 1963, 342). Therefore when we say "one," we mean "unity itself and unity is not divisible at all" (*Œuvres* 75.5–6; *Rasāʾil* 1:147, 10). One is thus not a number but the *measure* of number or, in other words, the *unit* of counting. As such it is also indivisible, since the unit "is what is taken to be indivisible for the purpose of counting." Not being a number, "one" does not fall under the category of quantity "but under another category." Without further specification, Kindī concludes:

> Thus "one" is not a number by nature, but equivocally (*bi-ishtibāh al-ism*), since numbers are not said except in relation to one thing: [just as] medical things [are said so] in relation to medicine and healthy things in relation to health. (*Œuvres* 75.9–11; *Rasāʾil* 1:147.14–16)

Before telling us what he means by such a definition, which reminds us of *Metaph.* IV.2, 1003a33 ff., and the many "senses in which a thing may be said to 'be,' but they are all related to one central point" (tr. Barnes 1984), Kindī still has to explore, in a sort of interpolation that interrupts the flow of the argument, further contradictions to which we will be led if we were to consider one as a number and hence as a quantity to which will apply equality and inequality, odd or even (*Œuvres* 75.12–77.14; *Rasāʾil* 1:147.17–149.5).

Kindī seems to have reached a dead end. He thus needs to resume and complete his argument:

> Since it has not yet been made manifest through this inquiry that one is necessarily not a number, we thus say: the element (*rukn*) of a thing, from which the thing is constructed—I mean of which the thing is composed—is not the thing itself. Like the articulate sounds of which a sentence is composed: as such they are not the sentence because a sentence "is a composite conventional sound, signifying something with [the addition of] time," whereas the letter is a natural incomposite sound. Hence if number is composed of units, as everybody agrees, then one is the element (*rukn*) of number and not itself a number. (*Œuvres*, 77, 15–20; *Rasāʾil* 1:149.6–11)

As already noted by Jolivet (*Œuvres*, 76 n. 62), this formula combines the Aristotelian definitions of sentence and verb in *De Int.* 4, 16b 26–27 and 3, 16b 6. More significantly it bears some similarities with *Metaph.* XIV.1, where Aristotle states that "one" is "some underlying thing with a distinct nature of its own" (1087b 33) and it is a "principle" (cf. also *Metaph.* V.6, 1016b18 ff.). Such a statement should be read in light of *Metaph.* X.1–2, where we find a fuller discussion of Aristotle's theory of "one" as not being a number but the measure of number. As noted by J. Annas (1976, 36), Aristotle stresses the analogy of the unit of counting to the unit of measurement, "For measure is that by which quantity is known; and quantity *qua* quantity is known either by a 'one' or by a number, and all number is known by a 'one.' Therefore all quantity *qua* quantity is known by the one, and that by which quantities are primarily known is the one itself; and so the one is the *starting-point* of number *qua* number" (1052b 20–25, tr. Barnes 1984). The parallelism brings out also a further point: "The measure is always homogeneous with the thing measured" (1053a 24), like the articulate sounds of which a sentence is composed, in the example provided by Kindī. "Likewise it is not necessary that one—because it is the admitted principle/element of number—be a number. Rather because number is composed of units, it [sc. number] is units" (*Œuvres* 79.13–15; *Rasāʾil* 1:150.15–16).

Consequently, Kindī can define number as "the arrangement of units (*naẓm al-waḥdāniyyāt*), the collection of units and the combination of units (*Œuvres* 79.21–22; *Rasāʾil* 1:151.1), this way echoing Aristotle's definition of number as "a plurality of units" (*Metaph.* X.1, 1053a30).

Having shown that one is not a number, Kindī concludes this first section by coming full circle (*Œuvres* 81–83; *Rasāʾil* 1:151–52): the section had opened with preliminary remarks stating that none of the predicates that are applied to quantities, like large and small, long and short, or many and few can be predicated in an absolute way; they are always said in relation to something, for nothing is said to be large or small just in itself, but by reference to something else. Kindī now closes with the very same remark, but expanding on his original statement in order to explain here what he means by "relation":

> Given that none of large and small, long and short, many and few are said in an absolute way, but they are said in relation (*bi-l-iḍāfa*), each one of them is only related to something else of the same genus, not of another genus. Like, for example, magnitude: if it is a body it can then only be related to another body, not to a surface and not to a line, or to a place, or to time, or to a number or to a statement. (*Œuvres* 81. 3–7; *Rasāʾil* 1:151.8–12)

We can compare bodies with bodies, surfaces with surfaces, time with time, but one cannot say, while talking correctly, that a body is longer than a surface. To number, it being a discrete quantity, the same will apply. Kindī therefore concludes, without any other form of transition, that the One in truth (*al-wāḥid bi-l-ḥaqīqa*) is not susceptible to be in relation to something of the same genus, and not even to have a genus in the first place. "Hence the true One (*al-wāḥid al-ḥaqq*) has no genus at all. And we have said above that what has a genus is not eternal and that what is eternal has no genus. Thus the true One is eternal and does never multiply at all, in no species whatsoever" (*Œuvres* 83.8–10; *Rasāʾil* 1:153.2–4).

The statement echoes the description of the eternal at the beginning of chapter 2 (see *Rasāʾil* 1:113, 1 ff.; *Œuvres* 27, 7 ff.), which now takes its full meaning as we see it here being applied directly to the true One. A description of the nature of the true One that mirrors every aspect of the description of the nature of the eternal in chapter 2 follows immediately.

2.10.2. The True One Is Not Said of Any of the Things of Which One Is Said

> [The true One] is not said "one" in relation to something else, since it has neither matter through which it would be divided, nor form composed of genus and species—for what is like this multiplies through what it has been composed of—nor is it a quantity at all, nor does it have a quantity, because what is like this is also divisible, for every quantity, or everything that has a quantity, is subject to increase and decrease. What is subject to decrease is divisible and what is divisible multiplies in a certain way.
>
> It has been said that multiplicity is in every one of the categories and in what attaches to it in terms of genus, species, individual, specific difference, property, common accident, all, part, and whole. Likewise "one" is said of every one of these[8] and therefore, the true One is none of these. (*Œuvres* 83.10–18; *Rasāʾil* 1:153.4–12)

The second section of the chapter thus reviews all aspects of reality that are said "one" but of which the true One cannot be said, because the unity they encompass is always mixed with a certain multiplicity. This is a theme we have already met in chapter 3.

Having enumerated all the ways "one" is said, Kindī recapitulates the whole discussion, following closely, but not entirely, *Metaph.* V.6 (*Œuvres* 93.4–95.1; *Rasāʾil* 1:159.3–160.3 and 1015b 16–1017a 5). In the course of the discussion he mentions, among the things that are called essentially one "because their substance is one," those that are analogically one because "they are related to one [thing] (*nisbatuhā wāḥidun*), like the medical things that are all related to medicine" (*Œuvres* 93.15–16 and 1016b 7), thus echoing the definition he had given above of the "one" being a number only equivocally since numbers are said in relation to one thing: "like medical things are said so in relation to medicine and everything which is healthy is related to health." At stake is the kind of unity that happens through the relation to one and the same reality. The same kind of unity attaches to the different modes of being, in relation to substance (see *Metaph.* IV.2, 1003b 1–3, where the same examples are used), knowing that Aristotle has frequently asserted that "one" has as many senses as "is."

Kindī seems to have that in mind when closing this section: "It is evident that existence (*huwiyya*) is said of every thing whose cause is the 'one.' Existence is thus said of what is enumerated by the species of the 'one' " (*Œuvres* 95.1–2; *Rasāʾil* 1:160.4–5). Here he is also paving the way for the conclusion of the chapter, where the true One is said to provide beings with existence by providing them with unity.

[8] Reading *hādhihi* instead of *baʿdihi*, as suggested by Ivry 1974, 105 n. 1, followed by Adamson and Pormann 2012, 86 n. 90, by contrast with *Rasāʾil* 1:153.11, who mentions that the manuscript has no diacritical points, and *Œuvres* 83.17.

2.10.3. True One above and beyond Any Description

The chapter culminates in what looks strikingly like a piece of negative theology denying from the true One any attribute at all. The absolute unity and simplicity of the true One precludes any description of its nature.

> It has thus been shown that the true One is none of the intelligibles: neither matter, nor genus, nor species, nor individual, nor specific difference, nor property, nor common accident, nor movement, nor soul, nor intellect, nor all, nor part, nor whole, nor some, nor one in relation to something else. Rather it is absolutely one and does not admit of multiplicity. It is not composed of multiple [things] either. . . . The true One has thus neither matter, nor form, nor quantity, nor quality, nor relation, nor is it described by any of the other intelligibles: it has neither genus, nor specific difference, nor individual, nor property, nor common accident. It does not move and is not described by any of the things that are denied to be one in truth. It is thus pure unity only (*waḥda faqaṭ maḥḍ*), I mean nothing else than unity, and every "one," other than it, is multiple. (*Œuvres* 95.3–14; *Rasāʾil* 1:160.6–17)

This passage seems to reflect two different traditions. On the one hand, it has been read against the background of the *Plotiniana Arabica*, of which several texts explain the absolute simplicity of the One as an exclusion of any other attribute (*ṣifa*). The first Cause is "above the attributes because it is the cause of the attributes" (D'Ancona 1995a, 139 and n. 74). The *Liber de Causis* particularly bears some striking similarities in terms of terminology as well as content with *FPh* (D'Ancona 1995b, 170ff.). On the other, it has been compared with the theological *tawḥīd* of the *mutakallimūn* and particularly the Muʿtazila as transmitted in Abū l-Ḥasan al-Ashʿarī's *Maqālāt* (Ashʿarī, *Maqālāt*, 155–56 and 483, quoted by *Œuvres* 109 n. 82).

However, the impossibility of any description of the true One and its necessary corollary, namely its absolute transcendence, did not prevent Kindī from considering the true One as the cause of unity and by the same token of the existence of all things, hence exposing himself to the criticism that will be addressed to him by Ibn Ḥazm. Indeed, the true One is the only One by essence. Therefore, unity, because it is an accident in all the things, is not only radically different from the true One but also requires a first Cause of unity in order to avoid a regression ad infinitum "since it is impossible that things be actually infinite" (*Œuvres* 95.22).

> Therefore, the first cause of unity in things made one (*al-muwaḥḥadāt*) is the true One, who did not acquire unity from something else because it is impossible that things dispensing [unity] to each other be actually infinite at the beginning. Hence the cause of unity in the things made one is the first true One and everything that receives unity is caused (*maʿlūl*). Each "one," other than the One in truth, is one metaphorically and not truly (*al-wāḥid bi-l-majāz lā bi-l-ḥaqīqa*). Therefore each one of the effects of unity (*maʿlūlāt li-l-waḥda*) goes from its unity to its nonexistence (*ghayr huwiyyatihi*); I mean that it does not become multiple insofar as it exists, but it is multiple and not absolute one, that is absolutely one that does not multiply at

> all and whose unity is nothing else than its existence. (*Œuvres* 95.22–97.3; *Rasāʾil* 1:161.8–14)

This difficult passage marks the beginning of the conclusion toward which the whole treatise, or rather the whole first part of *FPh*, was aiming. Kindī brings in the different theses he has developed in the previous chapters in as many steps toward this final conclusion, in which Neoplatonic concepts overlap with the demands of Muslim theology, giving room to a complex and original synthesis. It had already been shown that unity and multiplicity were inseparable in all sensible things, and Kindī had already hinted at the end of chapter 3 that the cause of the association of unity and multiplicity should be a different "loftier and nobler" cause that would be pure unity. We now learn that such a cause is the first true and almost ineffable One, whose unity is not acquired from anything else by virtue of the principle of the impossibility of a regression ad infinitum in the past as has been demonstrated in chapter 2. Everything else that receives unity is thus caused and called "one" metaphorically.

2.10.4. One in Truth versus One Metaphorically

It has been already noticed (Adamson 2007a, 53) that the fourth chapter shifts from the opposition between what is "essentially one" and what is "accidentally one," to the opposition between the "one in truth" (*al-wāḥid bi-l-ḥaqq*) and "the one metaphorically" (*al-wāḥid bi-l-majāz*) already introduced in the first lines of the chapter but looming more largely in the conclusion (*Œuvres* 71.2; 95.26; 99.1; *Rasāʾil* 1:143.15; 161.11; 162.14). The meaning, however, is not the same. What is metaphorically one is not only "what is both one and many." It is what receives its unity from the true One, and hence from God, as Kindī explains in the last lines of the chapter:

> Since what we intended to clarify in terms of distinction between the things that are one (*wāḥidāt*) has been shown, so that the One in truth, Dispenser, Creator, Almighty Supporter, becomes manifest, as well as what are the things that are one metaphorically, I mean *having acquired [unity] from the true One*, exalted is He above the attributes of the heretics. (*Œuvres* 97.20–99.1; *Rasāʾil* 1:162.13–15)

Every "one" that is not the true One is thus an effect produced by the first Cause. What is being emphasized here is the ontological inferiority of the "metaphorically one" that is granted unity and by the same token existence from the true One. In other words, the "metaphorically one" is not only what is always associated with multiplicity, it is what depends, for its unity and hence its existence, on the true One. Compare with *On the True Agent*, where Kindī contrasts the true Agent who is not acted upon and is the Creator and the Agent of the universe to "what is below Him, that is, all His creatures, which are called agents metaphorically and not in truth, I mean they are acted upon in truth" (*Œuvres* 169.13–14; *Rasāʾil* 1:183.9–10). Beyond the distinction between what acts without being acted upon and what acts and is acted upon, here as in *FPh*, what is in truth is in the first place what is proper to God, as opposed to what is "below Him" and is created by Him and hence can be an agent only metaphorically because in reality it is acted upon. In both instances, *ḥaqīqa* refers to reality, whereas *majāz* refers to a derivative reality (see Heinrichs 1984, 136; Gannagé 2015).

2.10.5. One, Being, and Creation

Unity in the sensible things is thus acquired from the true One and is therefore an affection (*athar*) and an accident in what is essentially multiple. Such a thesis is inspired by the Arabic version of proposition 3 of Proclus's *Elements of Theology* (Endress 1973, 244–45, who also mentions an influence of prop. 2). Furthermore, D'Ancona has shown that the same formulation occurs in the conclusion of the *Liber de Causis* and that the emphasis on the "acquired" nature of unity in the sensible things stems from the Arabic version/adaptation of proposition 3 rather than from the original Greek text (D'Ancona 1995b, 160 ff., for a thorough analysis of the relationship between *FPh*, the Arabic version of Proclus's *Elements of Theology*, prop. 3, and the conclusion of the *Liber de Causis*). This idea is one of the main points of the conclusion of *FPh*: the true One is that which dispenses unity to everything else without having acquired it from something else. Being pure unity that is never affected by any kind of multiplicity, it is thus the cause of what is essentially multiple and contingent.

Still another idea is looming here: unity is the condition of existence in all sensible things, in such a way that what loses its unity loses its existence, as the passage mentioned above has concluded (Jolivet 1979, 72, established a parallel between this passage and Proclus's *Platonic Theology* II 1; cf. also Endress 1973, 244–45; D'Ancona 1995b, 159). The true One is not only a principle of unity but also a principle of being. In other words the true One makes things exist by making them one (Adamson 2007a, 56). Indeed, a few lines above, Kindī had specified that in the true One and first Cause "unity is nothing else than existence (*huwiyya*)." He now carries the idea a step further: being "pure being," the first One brings things to existence "through His own existence."

> Every being-brought-into-existence (*tahawwin*) is thus only a being-acted-upon (*infiʿāl*) that brings into existence what was not. The emanation (*fayḍ*) of unity from the first true One is thus the being-brought-into-existence (*tahawwī*) of every sensible thing and of everything that attaches to the sensible. Each one of them exists when [the first true One] brings-it-into-existence *through His own existence.* (*Œuvres* 97.8–10; *Rasāʾil* 1:162.1–3)

In fact, both ideas are correlative and belong to the same doctrinal complex, namely that of the *Plotiniana Arabica*. One of the main characteristics of this group of texts is a conception of the true One as "pure being" that departs from Plotinus as well as Proclus (D'Ancona 1995a, 124ff., esp. 144). Such an idea originates in the denial of any attribute to the true One, which is thus reduced to "being only" (*al-inniyya faqaṭ*). It is explicitly stated, in passages of the *Theology of Aristotle* with no equivalent in Plotinus, that the first Cause creates "through its being only (*bi-anniyatihi faqaṭ*)" (cf. Badawi 1977, 161, 6–9, quoted by d'Ancona 1995a, 144 n. 95).

The same implications are to be found in Kindī's conception of creation, in the closing lines of the chapter, where the true One is finally identified with the Creator. Yet the religious concept of creation is still expressed in philosophical terms, even though the true One and first Cause receives some of the beautiful names of God.

> The cause of the being-brought-into-existence is thus from the true One who does not acquire unity from any dispenser, but is by essence one, whereas what is being-brought-into-existence (*yuhawwā*) is not eternal, and what is not eternal is created (*mubdaʿ*), meaning its being-brought-into-existence (*tahawwīhi*) is due to a cause. Thus what is being-brought-into-existence is created, and since the cause of the bringing-into-existence is the first true One, hence the cause of the creation is the first true One. The cause from which is the beginning of movement—I mean the mover—, is the agent. Hence, since the first true One is the cause of the beginning of the movement of being-brought-into-existence (*tahawwī*), that is of being-acted-upon (*al-infiʿāl*), it is then the Creator of all things being-brought-into-existence (*jamīʿ al-mutahawwiyyāt*). Since there is no existence except through the unity it contains, and since their being-made-one (*tawaḥḥuduhā*) is their being-brought-into-existence (*tahawwīhā*), it is thus through unity that the all (i.e., the universe) subsists (*fa-bi-l-waḥda qiwām al-kull*), and if the things being-brought-into-existence departed from unity, they would flow and pass away (*ghāra wa-dabara*) simultaneously with the departure, in no time. (*Œuvres* 97.10–18; *Rasāʾil* 1:162.3–12)

In the passage at stake the true One is said to be the "cause of the *beginning* of the movement of being-brought-into-existence," not of the movement itself. That seems a way to preserve the transcendence of the Creator and true One who initiates the movement without being affected by its laws. Bestower of being and unity, the true One creates, structures, and supports, through his oneness, a world to which He does not belong. Such is the conclusion of *FPh*, which does not tell us how God exercises causality over his creation. The few fragments of the missing portions of *FPh*, collected by Rashed and Jolivet (see *Œuvres* 113–33), hint to such a discussion, though they are too scarce to draw any conclusion. The issue is addressed in other treatises. For instance, in the prologue of his treatise *On the Proximate Efficient Cause* (*Rasāʾil* 1:215–16), al-Kindī indicates that he has addressed the topic of the eternity, the unity, and the oneness of God in *FPh*. Having thus already explained the remote efficient first cause that is God, he now turns to the proximate efficient cause, that is, the heavenly bodies, in order to explain the unity of God through His activity, namely the organization of the universe.

2.11. Conclusion

The fourth chapter, and by the same token the first and only part of the treatise that has reached us, ends on an emphatic note:

> Since what we intended to clarify in terms of distinction between the things that are one (*al-wāḥidāt*) has been shown, so that the One in truth, Dispenser, Creator, Almighty Supporter becomes manifest, as well as what are the things that are one metaphorically, I mean having acquired [unity] from the true One, exalted is He above the attributes of the heretics, let us now complete this section and follow it up with what naturally comes after, with the support of He who has complete omnipotence, perfect power, and overflowing generosity. (*Œuvres* 97.20–99.3; *Rasāʾil* 1:162.13–16)

These few lines and the passage they close (reproduced above) echo the prologue of the treatise, which has opened with the existence of a "true One, cause of all truth," now identified with the One, Creator and Providential God of the revealed religion. Al-Kindī thus comes full circle, closing a tightly knit analysis that deduces from the finiteness of the sensible world the existence of a Creator and the generation ex nihilo of the world (see Elamrani Jamal 1989, 656). In between, four chapters and an argument finely woven out of different doctrinal and philosophical traditions that are all reflected in this conclusion: while the notions of emanation, dispensation, and efficient causality of a first Cause reflect the *Neoplatonica arabica* that make room for a true One and pure Being creating through its being only, the concepts of movement, existence, and time hint to the Aristotelian conceptual framework that remained at work throughout the treatise alongside the Neoplatonic inspiration. Finally the dichotomy *majāz* versus *ḥaqīqa*, as well as the very last words accusing of heresy those who ascribe attributes to God, alludes to a Muʿtazilī background, for which the *tanzīh* is a direct consequence of the *tawḥīd* (Jolivet 1971, 109).

Al-Kindī's eclecticism, including his integration of theological questions within the fabric of rational philosophy, has been enough highlighted by the scholarship and does not need further emphasis.

Therefore, in closing I would like to address quickly the issue of the influence of *FPh* and the legacy of al-Kindī within the Arabic philosophical tradition. Ironically, the only substantial and straightforward trace of *FPh* in later philosophical work is a negative one. Almost two centuries after al-Kindī's death, the Andalusian scholar Ibn Ḥazm (d. 456/1064) wrote a refutation of *FPh*, addressing particularly the issue of the characterization of God as a cause, in which he reproduces large fragments of the text, including excerpts of parts that are no longer extant (see Daiber 1986a and 1986b). A further fragment, referring to "section 9" of *FPh*, has been transmitted, also in al-Andalus, by Ibn ʿAbd Rabbih al-Andalusī (see *Œuvres* 129–31). A refutation written by Yaḥyā b. ʿAdī in order to answer objections leveled by al-Kindī against the Christian dogma of the Trinity reproduces a thesis attributed to al-Kindī that might be extracted from an otherwise unknown short treatise, a "Refutation of the Christians and abolition of their Trinity on the basis of logic and philosophy," of which we have no other traces. The theses attributed by Yaḥyā to al-Kindī are along the same lines as chapter 4 of *FPh* and use the five "voices" of Porphyry's *Isagoge* (see *Œuvres* 119–27). Finally a short fragment from the *Muntakhab Ṣiwān al-Ḥikma* of Abū Sulayman al-Sijistānī, concerning the knowledge of particulars God has (*Œuvres* 133), to which one can add another small excerpt in al-Tawḥīdī's *K. al-Imtāʿ* (see *Imtāʿ*, 3:133), completes this overall meager picture of the direct impact of *FPh* on the philosophical tradition.

This being said, Peter Adamson has drawn the contours and main features of a more significant "Kindian tradition" that engages directly with al-Kindī's own work and that he identified as "a significant force in the intellectual milieu for about two centuries following al-Kindī's death" (Adamson 2007a, 12–20 and 2007b). Among its main figures are Abū Zayd al-Balkhī (d. 934) and Aḥmad b. al-Ṭayyib al-Sarakhsī (d. 899), of whom unfortunately no work has reached us, but also Abū l-Ḥasan al-ʿĀmirī (d. 992) and Isaac Israeli (d. ca. 907) (see Rowson 1988 and Altmann and Stern 2009).

What remains to be done is to trace the influence of al-Kindī on the major Aristotelian philosophical tradition represented by figures such al-Fārābī, Avicenna, and Averroes. The scholarship has so far contrasted al-Kindī with this trend, though as noted by Adamson (2007a, 12) they are all heirs to a tradition he has inaugurated, namely the integration of Greek philosophy into the formation of a genuine Arabic philosophical thought. His eclecticism and more so his engagement with Muslim theology, while at the same time conferring to his philosophy a real originality, have contributed to set him aside from the other major figures of Islamic philosophy. Still, he has addressed issues that were later on taken over and developed by this tradition, even if in an opposite direction, like, for example, the question of the creation of the world or the oneness of the first principle. Trying to unearth his influence, even when his name is not mentioned, will contribute to reintegrate him as part of a tradition he has initiated and that might bear his imprint more than has been so far acknowledged.

References

Adamson, P. 2002. "Before Essence and Existence: Al-Kindi's Conception of Being." *Journal of the History of Philosophy* 40: 297–312.

Adamson, P. 2003. "Al-Kindi and the Muʿtazila: Divine Attributes, Creation and Freedom." *Arabic Sciences and Philosophy* 13: 45–77.

Adamson, P. 2007a. *Al-Kindi*. Oxford: Oxford University Press.

Adamson, P. 2007b. "The Kindian Tradition: The Structure of Philosophy in Arabic Neoplatonism." In *The Libraries of the Neoplatonists*, ed. C. D'Ancona. Leiden: Brill, 351–70.

Adamson, P., and P. E. Pormann. 2012. *The Philosophical Works of al-Kindī*. Karachi: Oxford University Press.

Altmann, A., and S. M. Stern. 2009. *Isaac Israeli: A Neoplatonic Philosopher of the Early Tenth Century*. 2nd ed. Chicago: University of Chicago Press.

Annas, J., trans. 1976. *Aristotle's Metaphysics: Books M and N*. Oxford: Clarendon Press.

Ash'arī, Abū l-Ḥasan 'Alī al-. (*Maqālāt*) 1963. *Maqālāt al-Islāmiyyīn*, ed. H. Ritter, 2nd ed., Wiesbaden.

Badawi, ʿA. 1977. *Aflūṭīn 'inda l-'Arab*. 3rd ed. Kuwait: Wikālat al-Maṭbūʿāt.

Barnes, J., ed. 1984. *The Complete Works of Aristotle*. 2 vols. Princeton, NJ: Princeton University Press.

Craig, W. L. 1979. *The Kalam Cosmological Argument*. London: Macmillan.

Daiber, H. 1986a. "Al-Kindī in al-Andalus: Ibn Ḥazm's Critique of His Metaphysics." In *Actas del XII Congreso de la U.E.A.I. (Malaga, 1984)*. Madrid: Union Européenne d'Arabisants et d'Islamisants, 229–35.

Daiber, H. 1986b. "Die Kritik des Ibn Ḥazm an Kindīs Metaphysik." *Der Islam* 63: 284–302.

D'Ancona, C. 1995a. "La doctrine néoplatonicienne de l'être entre l'Antiquité tardive et le Moyen Âge: Le *Liber de Causis* par rapport à ses sources." In C. D'Ancona, *Recherches sur le "Liber de Causis"*. Paris: Vrin, 121–53.

D'Ancona, C. 1995b. "Al-Kindī et l'auteur du Liber de Causis." In C. D'Ancona, *Recherches sur le "Liber de Causis"*. Paris: Vrin, 155–94.

D'Ancona, C. 1998. "Al-Kindi on the Subject Matter of the First Philosophy: Direct and Indirect Sources of 'Falsafa-l-ula,' Chapter One." In *Was ist Philosophie im Mittelalter*, ed. J. A. Aertsen and A. Speer. Berlin: de Gruyter, 841–55.

D'Ancona, C. 2011. "Plotinus, Arabic." In *Encyclopedia of Medieval Philosophy. Philosophy between 500 and 1500*, vol. 2, ed. H. Lagerlund. Dordrecht: Springer, 1030–38.

Davidson, H. 1969. "John Philoponus as a Source of Medieval Islamic and Jewish Proofs for Creation." *Journal of the American Oriental Society* 89: 357–91.

Davidson, H. 1987. *Proofs for Eternity, Creation and the Existence of God in Medieval Islamic and Jewish Philosophy*. New York: Oxford University Press.

Endress, G. 1973. *Proclus Arabus, Zwanzig Abschnitte aus der "Institutio theologica" in arabischer Übersetzung*. Beirut: Orient Institut / Steiner.

Endress, G. 1997. "The Circle of al-Kindī. Early Arabic Translations from the Greek and the Rise of Islamic Philosophy," in G. Endress and R. Kruk (eds), *The Ancient Tradition in Christian and Islamic Hellenism*. Leiden: Research School CNWS, 43–76.

Endress, G. 2003. "Mathematics and Philosophy in Medieval Islam." in J.P. Hogendiek and A.I. Sabra (eds), *The Entreprise of Science in Islam*: Cambridge (MA): MIT Press, pp. 121–176.

Endress, G. 2007. "Building the Library of Arabic Philosophy Platonism and Aristotelianism in the Sources of al-Kindī." in C. D'Ancona (ed.), *The Libraries of the Neoplatonists*, Leiden: Brill, pp. 319–50.

Gannagé, E. 2015. "Al-Kindī on the *ḥaqīqa-majāz* Dichotomy." *χώρα* (*Chôra*) 13: 173–190.

Gannagé, E. Forthcoming. "Al-Kindī, Ptolemy (and Nicomachus of Gerasa) Revisited." *Studia graeco-arabica* 6 (2016).

Gutas, D. 2004. "Geometry and the Rebirth of Philosophy in Arabic with al-Kindī." In *Words, Texts and Concepts Cruising the Mediterranean Sea: Studies on the Sources, Contents and Influences of Islamic Civilization and Arabic Philosophy and Science Dedicated to Gerhard Endress on His Sixty-Fifth birthday*, ed. R. Arnzen and J. Thielmann. Leuven: Peeters, 195–209.

Hadot, I., trans. 1989. Simplicius, *Commentaire sur les Catégories : Traduction Commentée*. Fascicle 1 : *Introduction, Première Partie*. Leiden: Brill.

Hasnawi, A. 1992. "Kindī Abū Yūsuf Yaʿqūb b. Isḥāq." In *Encyclopédie philosophique universelle*, ed. A. Jacob, vol. 3: *Les œuvres philosophiques: Dictionnaire*, vol. 1, ed. J.-F. Mattéi. Paris: PUF, 655–57.

Hasnawi, A. 1994. "Alexandre d'Aphrodise *vs.* Jean Philopon: Notes sur quelques traités d'Alexandre 'perdus' en grec, conservés en arabe." *Arabic Science and Philosophy* 4: 53–109.

Hein, C. 1985. *Definition und Einteilung der Philosophie: Von der spätantiken Einleitungsliteratur zur arabischen Enzyclopädie*. Frankfurt am Main: P. Lang.

Heinrichs, W. 1984. "On the Genesis of the *ḥaqīqa-majāz* Dichotomy." *Studia Islamica* 59: 111–40.

Ibn Abī Uṣaybiʿa Aḥmad b. al-Qāsim. (*ʿUyūn*) 1882. *ʿUyūn al-anbāʾ fī ṭabaqāt al-aṭibbāʾ*. Ed. A. Müller. 2 vols. Könisberg: "Selbstverlag."

Ibn Ḥazm al-Andalusī, ʿAlī b. Aḥmad. (*Radd*) 1960. *Al-Radd ʿalā Ibn al-Naghrīla al-Yahūdī wa-rasāʾil ukhrā*. Ed. I. ʿAbbās. Cairo: Maktabat Dār al-ʿurūba.

Ivry, A. 1972. "Al-Kindī as Philosopher: The Aristotelian and Neoplatonic Dimension." In *Islamic Philosophy and the Classical Tradition: Essays Presented by His Friends and Pupils to Richard Walzer on His Seventieth Birthday*, ed. S. M. Stern, A. Hourani, and V. Brown. Columbia: University of South Carolina Press, 117–39.

Ivry, A. 1974. *Al-Kindī's Metaphysics*. A Translation of Yaʿqūb ibn Isḥāq al-Kindī's Treatise "On First Philosophy" (*Fī al-Falsafah al-Ūlā*), with Introduction and Commentary. Albany: SUNY Press.

Jolivet J. 1971. *L'intellect selon Kindī*. Paris: Vrin.

Jolivet, J. 1979. "Pour le dossier du Proclus Arabe: Al-Kindī et la *Théologie Platonicienne*." *Studia Islamica* 49: 55–75.

Jolivet, J. 1984. "L'action divine selon al-Kindī." *Mélanges de l'Université Saint-Joseph* 48: 313–29.

Jolivet, J. 1993. "Al-Kindī vues sur le temps." *Arabic Sciences and Philosophy* 3: 55–75.

Jolivet, J. 2004. "L'Epître sur la quantité des livres d'Aristote par al-Kindī (une lecture)." In *De Zénon d'Elée à Poincaré: Recueil d'études en hommage à Roshdi Rashed*, ed. R. Morelon and A. Hasnawi. Louvain: Peeters, 664–83.

Kindī, Yaʿqūb b. Isḥāq al-. (*Cinq Epîtres*) 1976. *Cinq Epîtres*. Ed. and trans. Centre d'histoire des sciences et des doctrines, équipe al-Kindī. Paris: Editions du CNRS.

Kindī, Yaʿqūb b. Isḥāq al-. (*Œuvres*) 1998. *Œuvres philosophiques et scientifiques d'al-Kindī*. Vol. 3: *Métaphysique et Cosmologie*. Ed. R. Rashed and J. Jolivet. Leiden: Brill.

Kindī, Yaʿqūb b. Isḥāq al-. (*Rasāʾil*) 1950. *Rasāʾil al-Kindī al-falsafiyya*. Ed. M. ʿA. Abū Rīda. 2 vols. Cairo: Dār al-Fikr al-ʿArabī.

Kindī, Yaʿqūb b. Isḥāq al-. (*Rasāʾil2*) 1978. *Rasāʾil al-Kindī al-falsafiyya*. Ed. M. ʿA. Abū Rīda. 2nd ed. 2 vols. Cairo: Dār al-Fikr al-ʿArabī.

Kindī, Yaʿqūb b. Isḥāq al-. 1987 (*Ṣināʿa*). *Fī l-Ṣināʿa l-ʿuẓmā*. Ed. ʿAzmī Ṭaha al-Sayyed Aḥmad. Cyprus: Dār al-Shabāb.

Marmura, M. E., and J. M. Rist. 1963. "Al-Kindi's Discussions of Divine Existence and Oneness." *Mediaeval Studies* 25: 338–54.

Nadīm, Abū l-Faraj Muḥammad b. Isḥāq al-. (*Fihrist*) 1871. *Kitāb al-Fihrist*. Ed. G. Flügel. Leipzig: Vogel.

Qifṭī, Jamāl al-Dīn ʿAlī b. Yūsuf al-. (*Taʾrīkh*) 1903. *Taʾrīkh al-ḥukamāʾ*. Ed. J. Lippert. Leipzig: Dieterich.

Rashed, R. 1993. "Al-Kindi's Commentary on Archimedes' 'The Measurement of the Circle.'" *Arabic Sciences and Philosophy* 3: 7–53.

Rashed, R., ed. 1997. *Œuvres philosophiques et scientifiques d'al-Kindī*. Vol. 1: *L'Optique et la Catoptrique*. Leiden: Brill.

Rashed, R. 2008. "The Philosophy of Mathematics." In *The Unity of Science in the Arabic Tradition: Science, Logic, Epistemology and Their Interactions*, ed. S. Rahman, T. Street, and H. Tahiri. London: Kluwer-Springer, 129–52.

Rosenthal, F. 1956. "al-Kindī and Ptolemy," in *Studi Orientalistici in Onore di Giorgio Levi della Vida*. Rome: Istituto Per l'Oriente, vol. II, 436–456.

Rowson, E. 1988. *A Muslim Philosopher on the Soul and its Fate: Al-ʿĀmirī's Kitāb al-Amad ʿalā l-abad*. New Haven: American Oriental Society.

Tawḥīdī, Abū Ḥayyān al-. (*Imtāʿ*) 1953. *Kitāb al-Imtāʿ wa-l-muʾānasa*. Ed. A. Amin and A. El-Zein. 3 vols. in 1. Beirut: al-Maktaba al-ʿaṣriyya.

Toomer, G. J. 1984. *Ptolemy's Almagest*. New York: Springer.

Walzer, R. 1962. "New Studies on al-Kindī." In R. Walzer, *Greek into Arabic: Essays on Islamic Philosophy*. Columbia: University of South Carolina Press.

Wolfson, H. A. 1976. *The Philosophy of the Kalam*. Cambridge, MA: Harvard University Press.

Zimmermann, F. W. 1986. "The Origins of the So-Called *Theology of Aristotle*." In *Pseudo-Aristotle in the Middle Ages*, ed. J. Kraye, W. F. Ryan, and C. B. Schmitt. London: Warburg Institute, 110–240.

Zimmermann, F. W. 1994. "Proclus Arabus Rides Again." *Arabic Sciences and Philosophy* 4: 9–52.

CHAPTER 3

ABŪ BAKR AL-RĀZĪ (D. 925), *THE SPIRITUAL MEDICINE*

PETER ADAMSON

Abū Bakr Muḥammad ibn Zakariyyā' al-Rāzī (251/865–313/925) is known above all for three things. First and foremost, his work as a doctor. Like Avicenna, he was well known both in Arabic and in Latin medical literature (in Latin he was known as "Rhazes"). His medical writings were somewhat less influential than those of Avicenna, especially the *Canon*. But al-Rāzī was a far more original and experienced clinician than Avicenna. It has been seriously questioned whether Avicenna even practiced medicine, as opposed to just writing about it. (For a defense of Avicenna having practiced to some extent, see Pormann 2013.) No one could have the same doubt about al-Rāzī. We are told that he directed hospitals in both his native Rayy and in Baghdad. He not only wrote lengthy overviews of medicine from a broadly Galenic point of view, but also collected his own observations of patients and how they responded to treatment. These observations, along with notes on Arabic versions of texts by Galen, Hippocrates, and other authors, are gathered into a text called *al-Ḥāwī*, or *The Comprehensive Book*. It is aptly named, filling no fewer than twenty-three volumes in a modern printed edition. He also wrote texts on more specific medical topics, including a groundbreaking treatise on differential diagnosis.

Al-Rāzī's second claim to fame is his philosophical theory of the "five eternals." With this theory, he explained how the cosmos derives from five principles: God, soul, matter, time, and place. Unlike al-Rāzī's medical output, which is extensively preserved, his writings about the five eternals are lost. The theory is therefore known to us solely through the reports of contemporaries and later authors. Our witnesses are usually hostile, and mention al-Rāzī only in order to refute him. It is easy to see why the theory provoked not just opposition but outright scorn. Al-Rāzī would seem to be putting four other principles on a par with God, by recognizing them all as eternal. His cosmology has God creating the cosmos from eternally preexisting matter, which consists of atoms. Place and time must be eternal, since without them there would be nowhere for the cosmos to be, and no moment at which the cosmos could start existing. Soul too must preexist the cosmos, since according to al-Rāzī, God would never have created our universe if left to His own devices. The cosmos we see around us is full of suffering, and cannot derive only from a wise and merciful deity. It must instead be the product of the soul's foolish choice to involve itself with matter.

The third famous aspect of al-Rāzī's intellectual life is his critical stance on prophecy. Again, for our knowledge of these remarks we rely on his critics, first and foremost Abū Ḥātim al-Rāzī, another man from the city of Rayy (hence both are called "al-Rāzī"). His *Proofs of Prophecy* (Abū Ḥātim al-Rāzī 2011) refutes a book about prophecy by our al-Rāzī. Abū Ḥātim also recounts face-to-face encounters in which al-Rāzī expounded his views on both the five eternals and prophecy. According to Abū Ḥātim, al-Rāzī (referred to here as "the heretic") decried supposed prophets as charlatans, who use tricks to persuade gullible religious believers that they can perform miracles. Al-Rāzī again invokes God's mercy and wisdom, insisting that He would never set factions against one another by giving them different leaders (*imāms*) with different revelations. There is room for doubt as to whether al-Rāzī's position is being accurately represented by Abū Ḥātim. Other evidence shows that he engaged carefully with theologians over the meaning of the Qurʾān, and in fact insisted that it agreed with his five eternals theory (Rashed 2008). But a number of figures apart from Abū Ḥātim, several of them Ismāʿīlīs like he was, agree that al-Rāzī was a heretical critic of Islam, and of revealed religion more generally (Stroumsa 1999; Vallat 2016).

None of these three aspects of al-Rāzī's thought—his medicine, his five eternals theory, or his critique of prophecy—is obviously on show in his longest surviving philosophical work, *The Spiritual Medicine* (*al-Ṭibb al-rūḥānī*; cited as *SM*, page numbers from al-Rāzī, *Rasāʾil*). At first glance it seems instead to be a rather conventional treatise on ethics. In the course of *The Spiritual Medicine*, we are lectured about the dangers of drink, advised on how to wean ourselves of envy and grief, and even told to stop fidgeting. Memorable anecdotes, quotations of poetry, and cautionary tales complete the picture of a work that belongs more in the self-help section of a bookshop than the shelves of a philosopher's library. Yet, underlying the popular and occasionally hectoring tone is a sophisticated moral psychology, which does on closer inspection relate to the rest of al-Rāzī's thought.

The most obvious connection is to his career as a doctor, as we can see from the very title of the work. As al-Rāzī explains in a prologue (*SM* 15; for translations see Arberry 1950 and Brague 2003), it is intended as a companion volume to a medical work entitled *Kitāb al-Manṣūrī*, or *Book for Manṣūr* (al-Rāzī 1987). The title refers to the dedicatee, the Samanid prince al-Manṣūr b. Ismāʿīl. The *Book for Manṣūr* provides a detailed exposition of medical knowledge, with a sizable introduction followed by discussions of bodily temperament or "mixture" (*mizāj*), nutrition, the maintenance of health, and so on for hundreds of pages that discuss everything from hair problems to the setting of fractures. As wide ranging as the *Book for Manṣūr* is, though, it covers only one type of medicine: medicine for the body (*al-ṭibb al-jismānī*). The *Spiritual Medicine* completes the project by dealing with the other type of medicine: medicine for the soul.

The relation of the *Spiritual Medicine* to the rest of al-Rāzī's philosophy is less evident. I will return to that question at the end of this chapter (section 3.6). First, I will (section 3.1) provide some context by considering the Galenic background of the idea that there is a "medicine for the soul." As we will see, al-Rāzī is not the only author in the Arabic tradition to make use of this idea. I will then (section 3.2) turn to the central theme of the *Spiritual Medicine*, namely the place of reason in the well-lived human life. This will be followed by (section 3.3) an examination of the most often discussed issue regarding the *Spiritual Medicine*, namely al-Rāzī's attitude toward the place of pleasure in the good life. That in turn will lead us to (section 3.4) a consideration of the limited aims of the work, which is intended only to help us tame and condition our lower souls, without necessarily achieving the well-grounded beliefs and superior values of the true philosopher. In light of this we will be able (section 3.5) to come to a better understanding of the relationship between the *Spiritual Medicine* and al-Rāzī's other surviving work on ethics, the *Philosophical Life* (*al-Sīra al-falsafiyya*).

3.1. Medicine for Souls

The notions that the philosopher is a "doctor of the soul," and that souls can become ill and require medical treatment just as bodies do, were widespread in antiquity (Pigeaud 1981). But Arabic ethical literature draws on one main Hellenic source for this theme: Galen. He draws the parallel in two ethical works that were transmitted into Arabic, entitled *On the Affections of the Soul* (Galen 1819–33, 5:1–57, trans. Galen 1997, 100–127) and *On Character Traits* (Kraus 1937, trans. Mattock 1972; cf. further Walzer 1949). At the beginning of *On the Affections of the Soul* Galen says himself that many philosophers, such as Chrysippus, have written on *therapeia* of the soul (Galen, *Affections*, 3). He carries on this tradition by defending a Stoic ethical ideal on the basis of Platonist psychology. We should, as the Stoics taught, learn to follow reason rather than "affections" (*pathē*), which give rise to "irrational impulses" (Galen, *Affections*, 7), and which may be understood as diseases of the soul (*nosēma psuchēs*, at *Affections*, 24).

Galen, however, rejects the Stoic doctrine that the human soul is rational through and through, and that affections like anger or fear can be understood as false beliefs. Instead, he invokes the Platonic conception of a soul with three powers or aspects (often called simply three "souls"; at *Traits*, 26, Galen characteristically says that we should not be fussy about the terminology). Only the highest of these three is capable of reason, and it alone is susceptible to "education" (Galen, *Traits*, 42). The lower souls are those that are shared with nonhuman animals, namely the spirited and desiring souls. Affections arise from these two parts, and are to be distinguished from failures of reasoning, which Galen instead designates as "errors (*hamartēmata*) that arise through false belief" (Galen, *Affections*, 7, cf. *Traits*, 30). Many, if not all, of our "character traits" (*akhlāq*) are seated in the lower souls (*Traits*, 25–26). These traits arise through inborn natural tendency or through habituation (*Traits*, 30–31), and must be combated by positive habituation or training, which will weaken or "tame" the lower souls to the point that they can be dominated by reason. For Galen, this is what it means to impose "health" on a soul.

A number of early Arabic texts can be grouped under the heading of "Galenic ethics" (see Strohmaier 2003; Adamson, forthcoming). We already find the first Hellenizing philosopher to write in Arabic, al-Kindī, composing a work called *On Dispelling Sadness*, which compares sadness to a disease (§IV.1 in the translation found in Adamson and Pormann 2012). But this most likely does not draw directly on Galen himself. For that, we need to wait until al-Kindī's student Abū Zayd al-Balkhī. As with al-Rāzī's *Spiritual Medicine*, the Galenic agenda is already clear from the title of al-Balkhī's treatise *Benefits for Bodies and Souls* (*Maṣāliḥ al-abdan wa-l-anfus*, facsimile text in al-Balkhī 1984; partial translation in Özkan 1990; discussion by Biesterfeldt 2012). As one might anticipate from the title, al-Balkhī divides his remarks into two sections, on the care of body and of the soul, with a transition devoted to the effects of music and poetry on both body and soul. The second part on the care of soul looks at various psychological defects or maladies, such as anger, sadness (this discussion resonates strongly with that of his teacher al-Kindī), and obsessive thoughts (*wasāwis*). The parallel structure to al-Rāzī's paired works, the *Book for Manṣūr* and *Spiritual Medicine*, is striking and perhaps no coincidence. We are told in the *Fihrist* of Ibn al-Nadīm that al-Rāzī studied with a man from Balkh, and it is possible that Abū Zayd is meant (Adamson and Biesterfeldt, forthcoming). Alternatively, both men were drawing independently on Galen's medicalizing approach to ethics. A further Galenic ethical work is the *Refinement of Character* (*Tahdhīb al-akhlāq*) by Miskawayh, which however adds Aristotle and other sources to the mix (text and translation in Miskawayh 1967 and Zurayk 1968). Its final section in particular adheres to the Galenic paradigm, stating explicitly that the soul too has diseases. Miskawayh even cites Galen by name in discussing the nature of character. The *Refinement* brings us full circle by concluding with a long quotation from al-Kindī's *On Dispelling Sadness*.

It is worth stressing that none of these works present the parallel between bodily and psychological maladies, or between medicine for bodies and for souls, as a metaphor or simile. Rather, the claim is that the soul can *literally* be healthy or ill, and that there is *literally* a kind of medicine for the soul. As I have argued elsewhere (Adamson, forthcoming), the texts just mentioned provide good grounds for this. For one thing, there are strong structural parallels between the two kinds of medicine. Psychological medicine attends to both the preservation and the restoration of the soul's good state, just as bodily medicine does for the body (see al-Balkhī, *Benefits*, 269–70; Miskawayh, *Refinement*, 176). Furthermore, both bodily and psychological medicine aim at preserving and restoring balance, harmony, or equilibrium. As al-Rāzī says:

> [Plato] holds that man should, by means of bodily medicine, which is the sort of medicine that is widely recognized (*maʿrūf*), and spiritual medicine, which is achieved by means of proofs and demonstrations, give equilibrium (*taʿdīl*) to the actions of these souls, so that they may neither exceed nor fall short of what is intended. (*SM* 29)

We will see, however, that the "balance" to be sought in the soul does not consist in an equal balance between the soul's various powers, as the body needs to have its four humors balanced in Galenic medical theory. Instead, the soul's balance or harmony is for reason to rule over the rest of the soul.

A final consideration that lends plausibility to the idea of "spiritual medicine" is that some maladies involve both body and soul. Al-Balkhī says this explicitly in the case of obsessive thoughts, which manifest in the soul but can arise from a bodily cause, namely an excess of yellow bile (al-Balkhī, *Benefits*, 323–23). The reverse is also true, in that maladies of the soul can cause bodily symptoms. Al-Rāzī remarks, for instance, that envy harms the body, "because upon the incidence of these symptoms in the soul, [the body] undergoes prolonged sleeplessness and bad diet, which are followed by poor coloring, bad appearance, and the disruption of the [humoral] mixture" (*SM* 51). For the idea that psychological phenomena have a physical realization, one might readily think of Aristotle's famous remarks on anger involving the boiling of blood around the heart (*On the Soul* 403a31, followed by Miskawayh at *Refinement*, 193–94). But a more robust theoretical basis was available to these authors from Galen's *That the Powers of the Soul Depend on Those of the Body*, which was transmitted into Arabic in a version that still exists today (Biesterfeldt 1972). One of Galen's favorite examples in that work is drunkenness, since it so clearly illustrates that even the rational soul is affected by a bodily state. Al-Rāzī may be thinking of this in chapter 14 of the *Spiritual Medicine*, which warns against first the bodily, and then the psychological, dangers of drink. Like Galen, he says explicitly that drink has an effect on the rational soul (*SM* 73). Given this mutual interaction of the body and soul, it seems justified to say that medicine cannot restrict its attention to the body alone.

3.2. The Rule of Reason

All this may seem natural enough to us today, since we too speak of "mental illness." Less familiar is the idea that *ethical* failures are not just defects of the soul, but its diseases. As already intimated, this means for al-Rāzī what it meant for Galen: the failure of reason to dominate a person's soul and thus to control that person's behavior. Both are drawing here on Plato's analysis of the soul, in the *Republic* and *Timaeus*, as having three aspects: reason (called by al-Rāzī either *ʿaql* or "the rational soul," *al-nafs al-nāṭiqa*), spirit (the "irascible" or "bestial" soul), and desire. Al-Rāzī explicitly presents this in the second chapter of the *Spiritual Medicine* as the view of Plato, though he adds that it can also be ascribed to Socrates (*SM* 31). Though that might suggest that al-Rāzī is thinking of the *Republic*, where Socrates is the main speaker, it is more probable that he is drawing on the *Timaeus* and, more specifically, Galen's presentation of that dialogue (see further Bar-Asher 1988–89). Galen composed a commentary on the sections of the *Timaeus* relevant to medicine, which is known to us in part through quotations from al-Rāzī. Galen's paraphrase summary of the *Timaeus* is also lost in Greek, but survives in Arabic translation (Galen 1951).

The influence of the *Timaeus* (by way of Galen) can be seen in al-Rāzī's general statement regarding the three souls:

> According to [Plato] these two souls, the vegetative and irascible, lack the special sort of substance which survives after the corruption of the body, like the substance of the rational soul. Rather, one of them, the irascible, is the whole mixture of the heart, while the other, the appetitive, is the whole mixture of the liver. The whole mixture of the brain, though, is according to [Plato] the first instrument and tool used by the rational soul. (*SM* 28)

The assignment of the three souls to brain, heart, and liver is found in the *Timaeus* (69c–71b), but not the *Republic*. Here we have another point that connects the *Spiritual Medicine* to al-Rāzī's medical interests, given the anatomical dimension of the Platonist psychological theory as found in the *Timaeus*. Indeed, if we glance at al-Rāzī's *Introduction* to the art of medicine, we find him again distinguishing three psychological powers, "natural, animal, and psychic," seated in the liver, heart, and brain (al-Rāzī, *Libro de la introducción*, §11). We may seem to have here a discrepancy in "Plato's" theory as presented by al-Rāzī. If reason is seated in the brain, then how can it survive the death of the body, as stated in the quotation above?

A closer look at the quotation reveals the answer: the lower souls are nothing but mixtures (*amzija*) of bodily organs, whereas the rational soul is not the mixture of brain but rather uses that mixture as its instrument (*āla*). Since the *Spiritual Medicine* is a work on ethics and not psychology, we get less detail about this than we might have liked. In particular, we might wonder how the rational soul will be able to function after death, once its instrument is gone. Unlike Galen, who is notoriously agnostic on the issue, al-Rāzī seems to be firmly committed to the survival of the soul without the body. He asserts, again speaking for Plato, that after the death of the body, the rational soul will still be alive and capable of reasoning (*nuṭq*, *SM* 31). We might infer that even in this life reasoning proceeds without any physical correlate in the brain. A list of the functions of the rational soul provided by al-Rāzī includes "sensation, voluntary motion, imagination, thought (*fikr*), and memory" (*SM* 28). A plausible conclusion would be that all the items on this list apart from thought do require the body, and more specifically the brain's mixture. These functions would then be unavailable after death (raising the question of whether we will remember our earthly existence in the afterlife).

But such a distinction between immaterially realized thought, and materially realized sensation, volition, and so on, seems to be ruled out by al-Rāzī's other writings. In the medical *Introduction*, he predictably makes sensation and voluntary motion dependent on organs such as the nerves. But he also says that the three "governing faculties" of the rational soul, namely imagination, thought, and memory, depend on the "psychic *pneuma*" and are located in the front, middle, and back sections of the brain (al-Rāzī, *Libro de la introducción*, §11.5). Elsewhere in this work al-Rāzī explains that bodily imbalance can undermine "thought" (*fikr*) and "reason" (*ʿaql*) (*Libro de la introducción*, §13.4). All this makes it pretty obvious that, in this life at least, thinking does involve activity in the brain. Even if we take on board the caveat that the brain or its mixture is the soul's "instrument" and not the soul itself, the problem remains. Either this instrument is a necessary tool for thinking, or it is not. If it is necessary, then it is unclear how the soul can go on thinking after death. If not, it is unclear what the brain contributes to thought while we are embodied, and why its impairment should impede thinking.

As already noted, though, this is not the sort of issue that we would expect to be investigated in the *Spiritual Medicine*. In fact, when discussing the fear of death al-Rāzī explicitly refuses to get into a proof of the soul's immortality, since it would need long discussion and call for "demonstration, not reliance on what others have said" (*burhān dūna l-khabar*) (*SM* 93; see further below, section 3.4). For the purposes of this work, what interests him about reason is not its fate after our death, but its primacy in this life. Although the psychological theory discussed above is ascribed to Plato, and not asserted by al-Rāzī in his own name, it is deployed throughout the *Spiritual Medicine* and clearly finds approval with al-Rāzī himself. The exalted status of reason (*ʿaql*) is already underlined at the very beginning of the work. In the first sentence, he calls reason the means "by which we achieve what is beneficial in this world and the hereafter" (*SM* 17). It is valuable not only because of the practical advantages it brings, for instance the building of ships and (of course!) the boon of medical knowledge, but also because we use it to know what is at first obscure to us. Here al-Rāzī mentions as examples astronomy and "knowledge of the Creator," which is the "most beneficial thing we can achieve" (*SM* 18).

Because reason has such a high value, it is wrong to subordinate it to desire. Rather the reverse: we ought always to "have recourse to it, take it into account and depend on it" (*SM* 18). The entire *Spiritual Medicine* is an exhortation and instruction manual for giving reason its proper supremacy. Galen remarks that someone who gives in to anger—that is, domination by the spirited or "animal" soul—is tantamount to a wild beast deprived of reason (*Affections*, 22–23). This comparison of ethically defective people to nonhuman animals appears repeatedly in the *Spiritual Medicine*, beginning with its opening sentences, which state that "it is through reason (*ʿaql*) that we are better than the irrational animal (*al-ḥayawān ghayr al-nāṭiq*)" (*SM* 18; see further Adamson 2012). As the key difference between humans and animals, al-Rāzī highlights our rational capacity to refrain from following the dictates of desire and spirit. The position is stated generally here:

> The man of intellect ought to impede and restrain them [sc. desire and nature], never giving them free rein without having first established and considered what will result, imagining and evaluating this and then following the preponderant course, lest he be pained when he thinks he will be pleased. (*SM* 22)

Al-Rāzī sometimes uses the word *rawiyya*, "deliberation," as a label for the rational capacity to consider a course of action and weigh its appropriateness before embarking on it. Animals lack this capacity, and we "should not be like beasts in unleashing action without deliberation (*iṭlāq al-fiʿl min ghayr rawiyya*)" (*SM* 56).

3.3. Pleasure

… what criterion, then, should reason determine whether or not a given … or action is worth pursuing? One answer has been given by L. E. Goodman, who in numerous publications argued that al-Rāzī is an adherent of the ethics of Epicurus (e.g., Goodman 1971, 1972, 1999, 2015). Historically speaking, this would be rather difficult to explain, since Epicureanism was little known in the Arabic-speaking world, if at all. (Our main Greek source, Diogenes Laertius, was not translated into Arabic, and of course Latin sources like Cicero and Lucretius were not available either; Goodman 2015 proposes other possible conduits.) Still, one should not dismiss the idea out of hand. After all, if al-Rāzī is clearly reproducing Epicurean positions, that would itself constitute evidence that information about Epicureanism was somehow available. According to Goodman's interpretation, al-Rāzī is a hedonist, but a refined one. Like Epicurus, he holds that the most pleasant life is achieved through moderation rather than indulgence. Thus Goodman remarks that he derives "a moderate asceticism from purely hedonic considerations," and that "unlike Plato, he remains unswervingly loyal to the hedonic principle as *the* ethical ground" (Goodman 1972, 32 and 34). If this is right, then al-Rāzī's answer to our question would be that one rationally chooses a certain action in terms of what will procure the most pleasure over the long term. This will often mean forgoing immediate opportunities for pleasure. As we saw above, animals are incapable of such self-restraint, since they do not deliberate but simply seize any opportunity for pleasure that comes along.

Certainly, the *Spiritual Medicine* contains passages that support Goodman's interpretation. For example:

> Desire and nature always call one to pursue present pleasures, and to choose them with no thought or deliberation (*min ghayr fikr wa-lā rawiyya*) about the result. They incite and hasten one on towards [the pursuit of pleasure], heedless of the painful outcome afterwards, or the prevention of [further] pleasure which is yet greater than what came before. For these two [sc. desire and nature] take a view only to their current situation, and nothing else, and they reject only the pain that harms them in this very moment (*waqt*). . . . For this reason, it behooves the reasonable person (*al-ʿāqil*) to impede and restrain them [sc. desire and nature], never giving them free rein without having first established and considered what will result, imagining and evaluating this and then following the preponderant course, lest he be pained when he thinks he will be pleased. (*SM* 21–22)

This looks like nothing so much as a recipe for maximizing pleasure and minimizing pain over the long run. But there is a problem with Goodman's interpretation, which is the abundant textual evidence showing that al-Rāzī considers pleasure to have no value at all (Adamson 2008; Goodman 2015, 165-6 actually admits that al-Rāzī denies the core ethical teaching of Epicurus, namely that pleasure is the highest good, but continues to maintain that there are powerful resonances between al-Rāzī and Epicureanism). He adheres to the teaching of Plato's *Timaeus* (among other dialogues, but the *Timaeus* is again his probable source): pleasure is not a good, because it requires the presence of pain or harmful states that are being removed as one is pleased.

Evidence for this can be drawn from reports concerning a lost work by al-Rāzī on pleasure (collected in al-Rāzī, *Rasāʾil*, 139–64). But the *Spiritual Medicine* itself contains the same teaching:

> Because harm and the departure from nature sometimes occur little by little over a long time, and this is then followed by a sudden return to nature in a short time, in this case we fail to sense being harmed, whereas the return to nature is abundantly clear to the senses, and so we call this "pleasure." So some uneducated people think that [pleasure] occurs without any preceding harm, and they imagine it to be separate and pure, entirely free from harm. But this is not the case. Rather, it is impossible that there be any pleasure at all (*battatan*) except to the same extent as there was a preceding harmful departure from nature. (*SM* 37)

The implication of this, as already emphasized by Plato, is that pleasure cannot be the good—because it by definition implies the presence of harm or pain that is being eliminated through a process that brings us pleasure. This is not to say that all such processes of restoration are pleasant—as in the *Timaeus*, we feel pleasure only when we are restored quickly, just as we experience pain only when we are harmed quickly. As for the natural state, it is always imperceptible, and involves neither pleasure nor pain (al-Rāzī, *Rasāʾil*, 150). In this respect it is like the state of health, which is likewise said to involve no pleasure (*SM* 66). Here, al-Rāzī's position is in vivid contrast to that of Epicurus, for whom absence of pain was not imperceptible but rather the highest possible pleasure.

Evidently, al-Rāzī is no more a hedonist than Plato. How then can we explain passages in the *Spiritual Medicine* like the one quoted above, in which he encourages us to think about the long-term balance of pleasures and pains involved in a given course of action? A revealing passage is found in his discussion of gluttony, which I quote at length, in part because it is fairly amusing and in part because it is crucial for understanding al-Rāzī's ethical stance:

> A man of Baghdad was eating with me from a big pile of dates that was before us. I stopped after eating a moderate amount, whereas he overdid it until he had eaten almost all of them. After he was full and stopped, when I saw him gazing after what was taken away from the table, I asked him, "aren't you done, and your desire stilled?" He said, "I'd rather be back as I was at first, and that this dish was only just being served to us now." So I said to him, "if the pain and torment of greed is not eliminated for you, even in [your] current state, wouldn't the right thing be to stop before you are full, so as to relieve yourself of the heaviness and bloating affecting you now from being so full, and the prospect of indigestion you might have, which would bring illnesses on you that would cause you many times more pain than the pleasure you have had?" I saw that he understood the sense of what I had said, that it would help

> him and had gotten through to him. Upon my life, this and other such remarks are of more benefit to someone who has not engaged in philosophical training (*riyāḍāt al-falsafa*) than proofs built on philosophical principles (*uṣūl falsafiyya*). For someone who is convinced that the desiring soul is connected to the rational soul only in order to get the body (which plays the role of a tool and instrument for the rational soul) what will preserve it long enough for the rational soul to acquire knowledge (*maʿrifa*) of this world, will restrain his desiring soul and hinder it from getting more than sufficient nourishment, since he sees that the goal and objective of nourishing oneself is not taking pleasure, but preservation, which is not otherwise possible. (*SM* 70–71)

This passage shows that the person who thinks rightly—the one who acts in accordance with "proofs built on philosophical principles"—is entirely unconcerned with pleasure. What he wants is *knowledge*. He eats only to keep himself alive so that he can keep acquiring knowledge, and grudgingly accepts the need to satisfy his desires for this reason. This might put us in mind of the "necessary desires" of Plato's *Republic* (558d–e) or, again a likely source for al-Rāzī's train of thought, *Timaeus* 69c–d, which speaks of "necessary affections (*pathēmata*)", including pleasures and pains.

Something else we learn from this passage, though, is that appealing to such philosophical principles is no good when we are dealing with people who think in terms of maximizing pleasure. Al-Rāzī's advice to the glutton presupposes a hedonist calculus, in which long-term pain is said to trump short-term pleasure. But this advice is offered only because it will convince the glutton to improve on his current attitudes toward food. Persuading him that pleasure is not worth pursuing at all is not on the table (so to speak), because the glutton is not a philosopher. He can only benefit from advice that fits into his hedonistic set of values. Accordingly, this is the kind of advice that al-Rāzī gives: don't overeat, because in the long run it will give you more pain than pleasure. Similar passages scattered throughout the *Spiritual Medicine*, which gave rise to Goodman's "Epicurean" interpretation, can be explained in the same way. They are aimed at a reader who still needs this kind of ethical advice, a reader who does think solely in terms of maximizing pleasure and minimizing pain.

3.4. A Regimen for the Soul

One implication of the interpretation just offered is that the *Spiritual Medicine* is not intended to turn us into philosophers. It is, rather, to set us on the right road, by helping us to habituate ourselves so that reason can gain the upper hand over the lower souls. To return to the idea that this is literally a medical work, we can say that al-Rāzī's advice is analogous to the prescription of a diet or exercise regime in the case of bodily medicine. The idea of a "regimen" or training for the soul, analogous to the regimen prescribed for bodies, is already mentioned by Galen (*Traits*, 34). In chapter 2 of the *Spiritual Medicine*, al-Rāzī similarly speaks of "exercise" (*tamrīn*) for the soul (*SM* 20) and of "adjusting" (*waṭana*) the soul to struggle against desire (*SM* 21), a process that is more difficult for some people than for others. The process means not just restraining oneself from harmful pleasures, but even abstaining from harmless ones in order to "exercise the soul" (*SM* 22). As al-Rāzī puts it at one point, his goal is simply to "improve the character traits (*akhlāq*) of the soul" (*SM* 20; elsewhere the term "character trait" is glossed with the term "habit," *SM* 32).

For this purpose, it is not necessary to instill philosophically well-grounded beliefs in the reader. Ideally, al-Rāzī would like us to accept Platonic theories about the nature of the soul, the afterlife, and similar topics, to pursue knowledge rather than pleasure (however long term). But for the purposes of the *Spiritual Medicine*, it will be sufficient if we accept his advice to the point that our lower souls are tamed. Thus, right after presenting his version of Plato's teachings on the soul, al-Rāzī comments:

> Let the reasonable person bear these ideas in mind with the eye of his reason, and make them an object of his concern and attention. But if from this book [sc. the *Spiritual Medicine*] he does not acquire the highest rank and status in this respect, then the least he can do is to adhere to the lowest status, namely to take the view of someone who binds desire to the extent that he does not subject himself to worldly harm in this life. (*SM* 31–32)

The *Spiritual Medicine* is thus revealed to be a carefully designed work, which alludes occasionally to the more exalted truths grasped by philosophers, but spends much of its time berating us for acting like animals. When we behave like beasts, pursuing pleasure without even considering the long-term consequences, we are falling below even the barely acceptable "lowest status" of someone who pays no heed to the afterlife, but at least uses reason to avoid painful experiences in this life and to maximize pleasure over the long term.

It is entirely consistent for al-Rāzī to try to *shame* us into attaining at least this bare minimum, for instance by comparing us to animals when we fail to reflect on our actions before undertaking them. Like Plato and Galen before him, he sees the spirited soul as a useful ally for reason in combating desire, and the spirited soul responds not to reason but to shame or insult. An interesting case is the advice he gives on the topic of fidgeting. This does not sound like a particularly promising context for philosophical insight, but al-Rāzī tells a story that is revealing of his moral psychology. In the anecdote, a king who constantly fidgets, by toying with his beard, is criticized for this by a bold (and courageous!) adviser. The king is furious, but stung into self-improvement by the "rage and haughtiness" in his irascible soul (*SM* 78). Elsewhere in the *Spiritual Medicine*, al-Rāzī describes anger as just another affection of soul that we must defeat—as so often, he says that people who give in to this affection without thought are like beasts (*SM* 55). He also repeats an anecdote from Galen, who spoke of his mother biting into a lock in rage when she couldn't get it open—this is a garbled mixture of *On Passions of the Soul* 16 (an enraged man who bites a key) and 40–41 (on Galen's bad-tempered mother). Despite the intrinsic irrationality of anger, though, people like the king can be aided by it. Anger is useful so long as it is provoked by shame for giving into desire.

Al-Rāzī, then, recognizes at least three stages of moral development. In the first, we are no better than beasts, simply giving into desire. The second stage is achieved not by philosophical reflection, but by taming the lower soul and even recruiting it to the service of reason. This is what is happening when we restrain our desires in light of a hedonistic calculus that pays heed to pain and pleasure in this world, or when we make productive use of anger at our own weakness in the face of desire. Al-Rāzī is explicit, though, that we should seek to "surpass the binding of nature and the struggle against desire, and go on to something different and very much greater" (*SM* 24). This higher goal is the one pursued by philosophers. Having completely subdued desire and spirit to the rational soul, philosophers are no longer motivated by pleasure, but nor need they go to extremes in avoiding pleasure (a point made in the *Philosophical Life*; see below, section 3.5). They place no esteem on the goods of the body that are pursued by the lower souls, whose close ties to the body are not just motivational but also ontological—as we saw, they are nothing but "mixtures" of the liver and heart. Thus the philosopher is already close to living in the way that awaits him after death (more on this in section 3.6). The *Spiritual Medicine* alludes to this third and highest level of ethical attainment, but is not really intended to bring us to it. Rather, al-Rāzī's aim is to move us from the first stage, where the soul is beset by the psychological illnesses caused by dominance of the lower soul (fits of anger, sadness, envy, etc.), to a second stage in which the reason controls the lower soul, but retains merely "second-best beliefs" about what is valuable. Notably, this person is still a hedonist, and must be led to do what is right by considerations of pleasure and pain, or by shame and embarrassment.

An illustration of al-Rāzī's differentiated approach is provided by the final chapter of the *Spiritual Medicine*, on the fear of death. His opening move here is one that has already been mentioned: he declines to give a thorough philosophical discussion of the afterlife. Instead, he will focus on dispelling the fear of death even for the person who believes the soul will die along with the body. The consideration he offers is, again, one based purely on pleasure and pain: "According to the statement of those [who deny the afterlife], after death no suffering (*adhan*) at all will befall man, since suffering is a sensation, and sensation belongs only to what is alive" (*SM* 93). Given that in this life we are subject to pain, from this perspective the nonexistence of death would in fact be preferable to our present life. He goes on to consider a possible hedonist objection: what about all the pleasure I'll miss out on by being dead? This is not a problem either, says al-Rāzī, because the mere absence of pleasure is not painful—only the unsatisfied yearning for pleasure causes suffering, and that again is something to which we are subject only in this life. Again, the result is that death is better than life even for someone who rejects the afterlife (*SM* 93–94).

All these considerations are examples of what I have called "second-best beliefs," and it is interesting to note how close they come to Epicurean arguments against the fear of death (on which see Warren 2004). The right way of thinking about death comes only afterward, as al-Rāzī concludes the *Spiritual Medicine* with a sketch of what might await us if we our souls do not die along with the body. There's good reason for optimism, since the "truthful law" (*al-sharīʿa al-muḥiqqa*) teaches that we will be given eternal blessedness, so long as we have led a virtuous life. Moreover, God will forgive even those who led less than perfect lives, since "He does not demand what is not in [man's] capacity (*wusʿ*)" (*SM* 96). It's characteristic of the *Spiritual Medicine* that the discussion of this second view is much briefer than the foregoing section, where he assumed that the soul dies along with the body. In fact al-Rāzī follows Plato in believing that the soul will live on. But he makes no effort to prove this here. Instead, he focuses on persuading us not to fear death, whether or not we believe in the afterlife. To put the point in the medical terms implied by the title of the work, al-Rāzī wants only to cure people of psychological maladies, including the fear of death. And this is something that can be achieved without actually turning people into philosophers.

3.5. The *Spiritual Medicine* and the *Philosophical Life*

But of course, al-Rāzī does have a conception of how philosophers should live. Again, the clue is given by a title, in this case *The Philosophical Life* (hereafter cited as *PL*, quoted by page numbers from al-Rāzī, *Rasāʾil*; English translation in McGinnis and Reisman 2007). Far briefer than the *Spiritual Medicine*, this treatise is a defense of al-Rāzī's own lifestyle from critics who complain that he is insufficiently ascetic. Broadly speaking, he defends a life of moderation, but touches in some detail on other ethical issues such as the benign treatment of animals (see Adamson 2012). Famously, al-Rāzī defends the life of moderation as the one endorsed by Socrates himself, albeit that the younger Socrates led a more ascetic life because of his excessive zeal for philosophy (*PL* 100). Al-Rāzī explicitly connects his discussion here to the earlier *Spiritual Medicine*, which he says provides the indispensable foundation for its ethical teaching (*PL* 101). He then declares the positive teaching that forms the basis for what will follow:

> We have a state after death which is praiseworthy or blameworthy, according to our way of life during the time that our souls were together with our bodies. The best thing, that for which we were created and to which we are led, is not getting bodily pleasures, but acquiring knowledge and acting with justice. These two things [sc. knowledge and justice] liberate us from this world of ours, to the world in which there is neither death nor pain. Nature and desire call us to prefer for the pleasure that is present, whereas the intellect frequently calls us to forsake the present pleasures for things it [sc. intellect] prefers. Our Lord, by Whom we hope to be rewarded and fear to be punished, watches over us and is merciful to us. He does not want us to undergo pain, and He hates injustice and ignorance on our part, loving our knowledge and justice. This Lord punishes those of us who cause pain and those who deserve pain, to the extent that is deserved. One ought not subject oneself to a pain along with a pleasure, when this pain exceeds the pleasure in quantity and quality. (*PL* 101–2)

Although al-Rāzī speaks as if this is nothing but a summary of what he said in the *Spiritual Medicine*, in fact the passage straightforwardly asserts the primacy of values that remain mostly in the background in that earlier text. Now we have a clear identification of knowledge and justice as the goals of human life. Pain and pleasure are still given some weight—we are told again how foolish it is to subject ourselves to pain if it outweighs pleasure, and God Himself is said to hate suffering, an attitude we should imitate by never causing pain to others. But what is really valuable is knowledge and justice, not pleasure, and what is really hateful to God (and to the philosopher) is not just pain, but injustice and ignorance.

It has sometimes been felt that there is a tension between al-Rāzī's two ethical works, in that the *Spiritual Medicine* seems to recommend an ascetic lifestyle, whereas the *Philosophical Life* defends a life that includes the moderate enjoyment of pleasures (Druart 56, following Bar-Asher 1988–89; Druart's solution is broadly similar to the one endorsed here). Whereas the *Spiritual Medicine* is constantly urging us to forgo pleasures, the *Philosophical Life* contains remarks such as this:

> We must not seek pleasure which inevitably involves committing some [deed] that would prevent our being liberated to the world of the soul, or which necessarily leads to a pain whose extent in quantity or quality is greater, and more intense, than the pleasure which we chose. But other pleasures apart from this are allowed for us. (*PL* 102)

The last sentence, with its defensive remark about the acceptability of pleasure, may seem to fit badly with the disdain shown toward pleasure in the *Spiritual Medicine*. But there too, we occasionally find him making the same point, as when al-Rāzī speaks of an "extent of restraining the desires" that "is sufficient" (*SM* 23). In both texts, then, we find the idea that the pursuit of pleasure is acceptable, even if it is not the primary goal of the philosophical life. The two works also agree about that primary goal: though the *Spiritual Medicine* mostly focuses on the task of restraining the lower souls, it does also speak about the higher values of knowledge and justice. We have already seen it allude to the value of knowledge in the passage on the glutton (*SM* 70–71). Justice comes up especially in the penultimate chapter, which however is very brief and consists mostly of an attack on people whose beliefs lead them into injustice (for instance Manichaeans; see further below, section 3.6). Tellingly, the chapter concludes by stating that these brief remarks are "sufficient for our objective in this book" (*SM* 92).

If there is a difference between the two works, then, it is more one of emphasis, which in turn derives from a difference in purpose. In both, al-Rāzī asserts that it is counterproductive to do things that bring more pain than pleasure in the long run. This advice takes center stage in the *Spiritual Medicine*, since it is trying to help us train ourselves so that we are at least better than animals, living in accordance with reason even if we fall short of a philosophical way of life in that our utmost motivation remains pleasure and the avoidance of pain. In the *Philosophical Life*, as one would expect given the title and the fact that al-Rāzī is stridently describing and defending his own way of life, the third, highest way of life is in focus. To live as philosophers, we need to embrace a more advanced set of values, preferring justice and knowledge even to harmless pleasure. True philosophers, like the mature Socrates, will enjoy such pleasures so long as such enjoyment does not undermine an unswerving commitment to knowledge and justice. Still, even a philosopher may forgo harmless pleasures for the sake of training the soul (*PL* 102; al-Rāzī again refers us back to the *Spiritual Medicine*, where he made the same point).

Before leaving this topic let me give one last, particularly memorable, example: sex. Al-Rāzī's discussion of sex in the *Spiritual Medicine* has the general tenor of an abstinence lecture. He summarizes his aforementioned view that pleasure is a mere restoration to the natural state, in an apparent bid to get us to stop pursuing it. There follow numerous warnings about the perils of love, including uncontrolled behavior even worse than what we find among beasts, and the misery visited upon the ardent lover that far outweighs any pleasure he can hope to attain (*SM* 39–40). In short, "The pleasure of sex is the most revolting and repellent of desires from the point of view of the rational soul" (*SM* 39). In light of this it is surprising to discover that in a medical work on sexual intercourse, al-Rāzī commends moderate sexual activity as beneficial for health (Pormann 2007). Turning to the *Philosophical Life*, we find him mentioning Socrates's fathering of children as a sign of appropriately moderate behavior (*PL* 100–101). He even mentions a reason why we should not be celibate: it leads to the "perdition of mankind" (*buwār al-nās*) by thwarting procreation. (For a response to this sort of accusation, see the work in defense of celibacy by the Christian Peripatetic thinker Yaḥyā b. ʿAdī, discussed in Druart 2008.) Again, the apparent tension can be dissolved in light of the interpretation offered above. The remarks in the *Spiritual Medicine* are aimed at someone who is weak in the face of sexual desires and needs to be trained, at least to the point of having these desires dominated by reason. But in a medical context, or in the context of discussing a genuinely philosophical life where training is already complete, al-Rāzī is able to commend moderate sexual activity.

3.6. The *Spiritual Medicine* and the Five Eternals

Having reconciled the *Spiritual Medicine* with the *Philosophical Life*, there remains the small matter of squaring it with everything else al-Rāzī said and wrote. As al-Rāzī might say, this would be a long discussion that would take us beyond the requirements of the present work. Still, we should at least briefly address the question of what relation, if any, can be found between the *Spiritual Medicine* and al-Rāzī's notorious theory of the five eternals. The theory is certainly never mentioned explicitly in either the *Spiritual Medicine* or the *Philosophical Life*. That might be another feature of these works explained by their limited aims—one that incidentally helps to explain why they survived, free as they were of his notoriously heretical doctrines. (This did not stop Ḥamīd al-Dīn al-Kirmānī, who like other Ismāʿīlīs was a staunch critic of al-Rāzī, from writing a refutation of the *Spiritual Medicine* called *Golden Sayings* (*al-Aqwāl al-dhahabiyya*).) Yet it would be disquieting if we could not at least reconcile these two sides of al-Rāzī's thought, since the theory of the five eternals is replete with ethical significance.

The theory is to a large extent motivated by the need to provide a theodicy (a point noted by Rashed 2008, 170). We have seen al-Rāzī saying that God hates pain (*PL* 101–2), and yet we find tremendous suffering in the world around us. In part for this reason, al-Rāzī postulates an eternal Soul in addition to God. Soul is in several respects similar to God—it exerts causality by emanating, and is an active principle contrasted to the passivity of matter (al-Rāzī, *Rasāʾil*, 197; Fakhr al-Dīn al-Rāzī, however, says that Soul is both active and passive, *Maṭālib*, 4: 213). Crucially, though, the Soul is in itself "ignorant" and can become wise only through the gift of reason or intellect (*ʿaql*) bestowed upon it by the Creator (al-Rāzī, *Rasāʾil*, 204). As Fakhr al-Dīn reports:

> [God], may He be exalted, emanated the light of intellect upon the substance of the Soul, so that, thanks to the light of intellect, it might become clear to [the soul] that the harms inflicted in this union [with body] are greater than the goods that arise in it. (*Maṭālib*, 4: 411)

The Soul's intellectual capacity for acquiring wisdom can be realized only through a learning experience, which teaches it the foolishness of involvement with matter. In a picturesque analogy, al-Rāzī compares God's attitude toward the Soul to that of a wise father toward a foolish son. Such a father might allow the son to wander into a beautiful, but dangerous garden full of thorns and stinging insects, in order to teach the son a lesson. In the same way, God allows the Soul to become involved with matter, even though He knows the suffering that will ensue (al-Rāzī, *Rasāʾil*, 309).

Our evidence concerning the five eternals theory does not tell us about the relation between this ignorant eternal Soul—which would seem to be a version of the World Soul from Plato's *Timaeus*—and the individual souls of humans and animals. Yet the idea that soul should pursue "liberation" from body is one that ties al-Rāzī's cosmology to his ethical treatises. A passage from the *Philosophical Life*, which has been taken to endorse a theory of animal-human transmigration, says that souls can be liberated only from human bodies. One reason we are allowed to kill savage animals is that it is "similar to the path towards and facilitation of deliverance" (*PL* 105; for discussion see Adamson 2012). The same work speaks of the eternal and unlimited pleasure that awaits us in the afterlife once we are "freed into the world of the soul" (*PL* 102). A bit further on, al-Rāzī describes this state as "eternal good and permanent felicity" (*PL* 103).

The same ideas can be found in the *Spiritual Medicine*. I have already quoted the statement that philosophers "surpass the binding of nature and the struggle against desire, and go on to something different and very much greater" (*SM* 24). This refers to liberation from the body, which can be achieved at least to some extent in this life, first through the restraint of desire and then through the pursuit of knowledge. Were the rational soul to "occupy itself completely with reason (*nuṭq*) it would thereby be freed from the body with which it is entangled" (*SM* 28). Of course death also promises liberation from the body. Speaking on behalf of Plato, al-Rāzī describes life after death as follows:

> [The soul] comes to be in its own world, and after this does not desire attachment to anything of the body at all. It remains by itself alive and rational, deathless and pain-free, happy with its position and place. Life and reason belong to it essentially (*min dhāt*), and it is kept apart from pain by being kept apart from generation and corruption. Its happiness with its position and place are due to its being liberated from the body, and from being in the bodily world. (*SM* 30)

Al-Rāzī adds, however, that the soul that has not learned to disdain bodily things in this life, and has not achieved "true knowledge" of the bodily world, will continue to be attached to bodies after death. In an apparent reference to Plato's belief in reincarnation, al-Rāzī says that this will subject the soul to continued pain, because of the generation and corruption of the body in which it resides (*SM* 31).

Another theme that shows up in both the five eternals theory and al-Rāzī's extant ethical writings is an emphasis on God's wisdom, mercy, and justice. We have already seen that the Razian cosmology introduces an ignorant soul to explain the presence of suffering in the world. This also helps him solve the problem of why the cosmos started to exist when it did, rather than at some other moment. The impossibility of God's arbitrarily choosing a time for the cosmos to begin is a standard late ancient argument for the world's eternity, and will play a significant role in al-Ghazālī's *Incoherence of the Philosophers* (see further Adamson 2016). Al-Rāzī's theory seems simply to presuppose that the cosmos is not eternal (see, however, his discussion of the question at the beginning of his *Doubts about Galen*, translated in McGinnis and Reisman 2007). Yet for God to create at an arbitrary moment would be incompatible with His wisdom. The arbitrariness of such an act can be likened to someone fidgeting with his beard (Fakhr al-Dīn, *Maṭālib*, 4: 405 and 408), an example of foolish behavior also singled out in the *Spiritual Medicine*, as we have seen.

Instead, the ignorant Soul must have provoked the world's creation by suddenly, and foolishly, conceiving a desire to be entangled with matter (al-Rāzī, *Rasāʾil*, 207–11, Fakhr al-Dīn, *Maṭālib*, 4: 411). God's response to this unfortunate event is said by al-Rāzī to be an instance of His wisdom and mercy. We have already seen him comparing God to a wise father who allows his child to learn the lesson of self-destructive behavior. But God is also merciful, and as we have seen emanates the power of reason or intellect onto the Soul in order to help it to liberate itself from matter. In His wisdom and mercy, He also bestows forms on things in the cosmos in order to make them as good as they can be (al-Rāzī, *Rasāʾil*, 205), even though matter is not capable of perfect reception of Soul and form (Fakhr al-Dīn, *Maṭālib*, 4: 411).

Of al-Rāzī's two ethical works, it is the shorter *Philosophical Life* that more clearly invokes these themes of divine mercy, justice, and wisdom. He follows the Platonic precept that we ought to seek "likeness to God" (Plato, *Theaetetus* 176b; see Druart 1997, 53–56). The person who most imitates God is the one who is "the most knowing, just, merciful and benevolent" (*PL* 108). As a concrete example of human benevolence, al-Rāzī gives the example of benign treatment of animals (*PL* 104–5, cf. Adamson 2012). By contrast, extreme ascetics, like certain Hindus and Manichaeans, depart from the imitation of God when they voluntarily inflict pain on themselves or renounce sex through castration. Even some Muslims go to excess in this respect (*PL* 106). Since pain is hateful to God, these attempts at purity are wholly misconceived—to deliberately seek out suffering is in fact to thwart God's will.

Although the *Spiritual Medicine* has somewhat less to say about these matters, there are clear signs that here too the best, philosophical life both is facilitated by God's mercy and is an imitation of God's mercy. Here we should recall the opening passage (*SM* 17–19), which extols intellect or reason (*ʿaql*) as a gift of God—exactly as the five eternals theory would have it. Another relevant passage is found toward the end of the treatise:

> The way of life (*sīra*) taken up and pursued by the virtuous philosophers is, to put it in a nutshell, acting towards men with justice. Beyond that, it is behaving towards them with virtue, showing continence, mercy, and good counsel towards all and exerting oneself to aid all, apart from anyone who has set out on a course of injustice and evil. (*SM* 91)

Much as he criticized religious sects for their excessive asceticism in the *Philosophical Life*, here al-Rāzī proceeds to attack the Dayṣaniyya, the Muḥammira (a subgroup of the Khurramiyya), and again the Manichaeans (*SM* 91). These groups have religious beliefs that actually require them to be unjust or unmerciful to their fellow man. The Manichaeans, for instance, withhold food and medical treatment from those who are not members of their sect. Al-Rāzī adds that it is in our own interest to show benevolence. If we benefit others, we can expect that they will return the favor (*SM* 92). This looks to be another case of the "second-best beliefs" characteristic of the *Spiritual Medicine*. A philosopher presumably displays mercy for its own sake and in imitation of God, not out of self-interest.

These passages show that, contrary to initial appearances, the *Spiritual Medicine* and *Philosophical Life* are indeed consistent with the five eternals theory, and even animated by the same central concerns. Underlying the popular tone of the *Spiritual Medicine* is not only a well-worked-out psychological theory derived from Plato and Galen, but an ethical theory that makes a godlike life of reason and mercy our ultimate goal. This may be too much to ask of most readers, and al-Rāzī admits that it is a standard he himself cannot always meet. In the *Philosophical Life*, he confesses to shortcomings and remarks that he would not presume to claim the title of "philosophy" for his way of life, at least not in comparison to a true sage like Socrates (*PL* 100–101). In the same breath, though, al-Rāzī claims to lead a philosophical life in comparison to those who are not pursuing philosophy at all. This is what puts him in a position to offer medicine for other people's souls, as well as their bodies—his way of showing benevolence in imitation of God.

References

Abū Bakr al-Rāzī. (*Libro de la introducción*) 1979. *Libro de la introducción dal arte de la medicina o "Isagoge"*. Ed. and trans. M. Vasquéz de Benito. Salamanca: Istituto Hispano-Arabe de Cultura.

Abū Bakr al-Rāzī. (*Rasāʾil*) 1939. *Rasāʾil falsafiyya* (*Opera philosophica*). Ed. P. Kraus. Cairo: Barbey.

Abū Ḥātim al-Rāzī. 2011. *The Proofs of Prophecy*. Trans. T. Khalidi. Provo, UT: Brigham Young University Press.

Abū Zayd al-Balkhī. 1984. *Sustenance for Body and Soul (Maṣāliḥ al-Abdan wa-l-Anfus)*. Frankfurt am Main: Institute for the History of Arabic Islamic Science.

Adamson, P. 2008. "Platonic Pleasures in Epicurus and al-Rāzī." In *In the Age of al-Fārābī: Arabic Philosophy in the Fourth/Tenth Century*, ed. P. Adamson. London: Warburg Institute, 71–94.

Adamson, P. 2010. "The Arabic Tradition." In *The Routledge Companion to Ethics*, ed. J. Skorupski. London: Routledge, 63–75.

Adamson, P. 2012. "Abū Bakr al-Rāzī on Animals." *Archiv für Geschichte der Philosophie* 94: 249–73.

Adamson, P. 2016. "Eternity in Medieval Philosophy." In *Eternity*, ed. Y. Melamed. Oxford: Oxford University Press, 75–116.

Adamson, P. Forthcoming. "Health in Arabic Ethical Works." In *Health*, ed. P. Adamson. Oxford: Oxford University Press.

Adamson, P. and H. H. Biesterfeldt. Forthcoming. "The Consolations of Philosophy: Abū Zayd al Balḫī and Abū Bakr al-Rāzī on Sorrow and Anger." In *Medicine and Philosophy in the Islamic World*, ed. P. Adamson and P. E. Pormann. London: Warburg Institute.

Adamson, P., and P. E. Pormann, trans. 2012. *The Philosophical Works of al-Kindī*. Karachi: Oxford University Press.

Arberry, A. J. 1950. *The Spiritual Physick of Rhazes*. London: John Murray.

Bar-Asher, M.-M. 1988–89. "Quelques aspects de l'éthique d'Abū Bakr al-Rāzī et ses origines dans l'oeuvre de Galien." *Studia Islamica* 69: 5–83, 70: 119–47.

Biesterfeldt, H. H. 1972. *Galens Traktat Dass die Kräfte der Seele den Mischungen des Körpers Folgen—in arabischer Übersetzung*. Wiesbaden: Franz Steiner.

Biesterfeldt, H. H. 2012. "Abū Zayd al-Balḫī." In *Grundriss der Geschichte der Philosophie: 8.–10. Jahrhundert*, ed. U. Rudolph. Basel: Schwabe, 156–67.

Brague, R., trans. 2003. *Al-Razi: La médecine spirituelle*. Paris: Flammarion.

Druart, T.-A. 1997. "The Ethics of al-Rāzī." *Medieval Philosophy and Theology* 5: 47–71.

Druart, T.-A. 2008. "An Arab Christian Philosophical Defense of Religious Celibacy against its Islamic Condemnation: Yaḥyā ibn ʿAdī." In *Chastity: A Study in Perception, Ideals, Opposition*, ed. N. Van Deusen. Leiden: Brill, 77–85.

Fakhr al-Dīn al-Rāzī. (*Maṭālib*) 1407/1987. *Al-Maṭālib al-ʿāliyya*. Ed. A. Ḥ. al-Saqqā. 9 vols. Beirut: Dar al-Kitāb al-ʿArabī.

Galen. 1819–33. *Opera Omnia*. Ed. C. G. Kühn. 20 vols. Leipzig: C. Cnobloch.

Galen. 1951. *Compendium Timaei Platonis*. Ed P. Kraus and R. Walzer. London: Warburg Institute.

Galen. 1997. *Selected Works*. Trans. P. Singer. Oxford: Oxford University Press.

Goodman, L. E. 1971. "The Epicurean Ethic of Muḥammad Ibn Zakariyāʾ ar-Rāzī." *Studia Islamica* 34: 5–26.

Goodman, L. E. 1972. "Rāzī's Psychology." *Philosophical Forum* 4: 26–48.

Goodman, L. E. 1999. "Rāzī and Epicurus." In L. E. Goodman, *Jewish and Islamic Philosophy: Crosspollinations in the Classical Age*. Edinburgh: Edinburgh University Press, 35–67.

Goodman, L. E. 2015. "How Epicurean was Rāzī?" *Studia graeco-arabica* 5: 247–80.

Ḥamid al-Din al-Kirmāni. (*Aqwāl*) 1977. *Al-Aqwāl al-dhahabiyya*. Ed. S. al-Sāwi. Tehran: Imperial Iranian Academy of Philosophy.

Kraus, P. 1937. "*Kitāb al-aḫlāq li-Jālīnūs*" [*On Character Traits*, by Galen]. *Bulletin of the Faculty of Arts of the University of Egypt* 5: 1–51.

Mattock, J. N. 1972. "A Translation of the Arabic Epitome of Galen's Book *Peri Ethon*." In *Islamic Philosophy and the Classical Tradition: Essays Presented by His Friends and Pupils to Richard Walzer on His Seventieth Birthday*, ed. S. M. Stern, A. Hourani, and V. Brown. Columbia: University of South Carolina Press, 235–60.

McGinnis, J., and D. C. Reisman, eds. and trans. 2007. *Classical Arabic Philosophy: An Anthology of Sources*. Indianapolis: Hackett.

Miskawayh. (*Tahdhīb*) 1967. *Tahdhīb al-akhlāq*. Ed. C. Zurayk. Beirut: American University of Beirut.

Özkan, Z. 1990. *Die Psychomatik bei Abū Zaid al-Balḫī (gest. 934 AD)*. Frankfurt am Main: Institute for the History of Arabic Islamic Science.

Pigeaud, J. 1981. *La maladie de l'âme: Étude sur la relation de l'âme et du corps dans la tradition médico-philosophique antique*. Paris: Belles Lettres.

Pormann, P. E. 2007. "Al-Rāzī (d. 925) on the Benefits of Sex: A Clinician Caught between Philosophy and Medicine." In *O Ye Gentlemen: Arabic Studies on Science and Literary Culture, in Honour of Remke Kruk*, ed. A. Vrolijk and J. P. Hogendijk. Leiden: Brill, 115–27.

Pormann, P. E. 2013. "Avicenna on Medical Practice, Epistemology, and the Physiology of the Inner Senses." In *Interpreting Avicenna: Critical Essays*, ed. P. Adamson. Cambridge: Cambridge University Press, 91–108.

Rashed, M. 2008. "Abū Bakr al-Rāzī et la prophétie." *Mélanges de la Institute Dominicain d'Etudes Orientales du Caire* 27: 169–82.

Strohmaier, G. 2003. "Die Ethik Galens und ihre Rezeption in der Welt des Islams." In *Galien et la Philosophie*, ed. J. Barnes and J. Jouanna. Vandoeuvres: Fondation Hardt, 307–29.

Stroumsa, S. 1999. *Freethinkers of Medieval Islam: Ibn al-Rāwandī, Abū Bakr al-Rāzī, and Their Impact on Islamic Thought*. Leiden: Brill.

Vallat, P. 2016. "Between Hellenism, Islam and Christianity: Abū Bakr al-Rāzī and his Controversies with Contemporary Muʿtazilite Theologians as Reported by the Ashʿarite Theologian and Philosopher Fakhr al-Dīn al-Rāzī." In *Ideas in Motion in Baghdad and Beyond*, ed. D. Janos. Leiden: Brill, 178–220.

Walzer, R. 1949. "New Light on Galen's Moral Philosophy." *Classical Quarterly* 43: 82–96.

Warren, J. 2004. *Facing Death: Epicurus and His Critics*. Oxford: Oxford University Press.

Zurayk, C., trans. 1968. *Miskawayh: The Refinement of Character*. Beirut: American University of Beirut.

CHAPTER 4

IBN MASARRA'S (D. 931) THIRD BOOK

SARAH STROUMSA

THIS chapter is dedicated to a book we do not have. Muslim sources tell us of several books written by the tenth-century Andalusī thinker Muḥammad Ibn Masarra, but so far only two books identified with certainty as his are known to be extant. In what follows, I will briefly review the evidence regarding Ibn Masarra and his books, then focus on a quotation from a third book, preserved in another source. I will analyze this quotation, and attempt to gauge from it how it stands in relation to what we already know, from other sources, of Ibn Masarra's thought. This somewhat speculative exercise has a double purpose: to draw a profile of this third book in the hope that, in case it happens to have been preserved in some manuscript collection under a different guise, this profile will enhance the chances of scholars to identify it and bring it to light; and to address through this analysis some of the open issues regarding Ibn Masarra's thought and its impact on Andalusī philosophy.

4.1. IBN MASARRA AND HIS BOOKS

Muḥammad b. ʿAbd Allāh b. Najīḥ Ibn Masarra (269/883–319/931) is commonly considered to have been the first Andalusī Muslim thinker of local extraction. Born in Cordoba, he was first educated by his own father ʿAbd Allāh, as well as by Muḥammad Ibn Waḍḍāḥ (d. 287/900) and by al-Khushanī (whose date of death is recorded as 371/981 or 361/971. Ibn al-Faraḍī, *Taʾrīkh*, II, 4; al-Dhahabī, *Taʾrīkh*, 590; Addas 1992, 913–14; Pellat 1986; Brown 2006b, 51). Like his father before him, he traveled to the East before returning to al-Andalus. He is known to have studied Mālikī law, and some of our sources add to his name the epithet "the jurist" (*al-faqīh*). He spent some time in Qayrawān (Khushanī, *Ṭabaqāt*, 159–60) and in Mecca. In Mecca he may have been associated with the circle of Abū Saʿīd b. al-Aʿrābī, an erstwhile disciple of the Baghdādī mystic al-Junayd, and perhaps with the circle of Muḥammad b. Sālim al-Tustarī, the so-called *Sālimiyya* (Morris 1973, 14–15; Marín 1992; Ebstein and Sviri 2011, 5, 10–11). Another indication of Ibn Masarra's closeness to these circles is the fact that the only Ṣūfī author quoted by name in his *Book of Letters* is Sahl al-Tustarī. Although the *Book of Letters* attributed to Sahl from which he quotes was shown to be a pseudoepigraph, it does indicate Ibn Masarra's participation in the emerging Andalusī Tustarian tradition (Ebstein and Sviri 2011). Upon returning to al-Andalus during the reign of ʿAbd al-Raḥmān III *al-Nāṣir* (r. 300/912–350/961) Ibn Masarra withdrew, together with some disciples, to the Cordoban Sierra (hence his appellation *al-jabalī*), and apparently stayed there until his death.[1]

Some twenty years after Ibn Masarra's death, there began an orchestrated public attack on those who were supposedly his followers. The public denunciation and harassment of the so-called Masarrīs (somewhat exaggeratedly presented in modern scholarship as persecution) came in several waves, beginning in 340/952 under the caliph ʿAbd al-Raḥmān III and continuing in 350/961, under al-Ḥakam II, as well as in 381/991, under al-Manṣūr Ibn Abī ʿĀmir. The Masarriyya—a term used only by Ibn Ḥazm, and perhaps, as suggested by James Morris, coined by him—were variously accused of upholding belief in the createdness of the Qurʾān, disseminating disputations concerning God's verses (*āyāt Allāh*), denying the [possibility of] repentance, denying the possibility of the Prophet's intercession, and casting doubt on the *ḥadīth* (Ibn Ḥayyān, *Muqtabas*, 20 ff.; Morris 1973, 12, 17–18, 26–27; Cruz-Hernández 1981; Fierro 1999, 180–84; Fierro 2012, 131–44; Safran 2013, 72–73). Of particular interest is Ismāʿīl al-Ruʿaynī, whose views were rejected by other Masarrīs, and who is said to have claimed the possibility to attain prophecy (*iktisāb al-nubuwwa*), a claim that some of the Masarrīs attributed also to Ibn Masarra himself (Ibn Ḥazm, *Fiṣal*, V, 67). It is not at all clear to what extant those described as Masarrīs can indeed be seen as disciples of Ibn Masarra, but the edicts that were read in the mosques against them can be helpful in reconstructing Ibn Masarra's image and are indicative of the impact that the doctrines associated with him had in contemporary al-Andalus.

Ibn Masarra's own writings were considered lost until 1972, when Muḥammad Kamāl Ibrāhīm Jaʿfar discovered two of his works in manuscript no. 3168 of the Chester Beatty Collection.[2] These treatises, which were subsequently published and analyzed, by Jaʿfar and then others, brought to an end much of the previous scholarly speculations regarding the nature of Ibn Masarra's thought. They amply demonstrate that Ibn Masarra was neither a Muʿtazilite nor an Aristotelian philosopher, and prove the unquestionably Neoplatonic nature of his philosophical mysticism.[3]

[1] For Ibn Masarra's biography, see Asín Palacios 1914; Morris 1973, 8–19; Brown 2006b, 39–92; Arnaldez 1986 (who weaves the scant information in our sources into a smooth, but not necessarily reliable, narrative); Ramón Guerrero and Garrido Clemente 2006, 144–46.

[2] Arberry 1955–1966, I, 68–69. The manuscript is a compendium of mystical and magical works, copied in Egypt in the late thirteenth century and including works by various authors.

[3] For scholarly evaluations of Ibn Masarra's thought, see Asín Palacios 1978; Morris 1973; Cruz Hernández 1996, 344–52; Tornero 1993; Addas 1992, 913–19; Stroumsa 2006; Stroumsa and Sviri 2009, 210

Ibn Masarra was apparently a gifted speaker, although not necessarily in the sense of being a fiery orator. Our sources describe him as a very effective conversationalist, someone who had a way with words ("*ṭarīqa fī l-balāgha*"), whose charismatic personality made a powerful impression on people and attracted to him disciples (al-Ḥumaydī, *Jadhwa*, 58; also Ibn ʿIdhārī, *Bayān*, 195). An example of the way he talked is preserved by al-Khushanī, who attended in Qayrawān a meeting between the young Ibn Masarra and the famous Mālikī jurist Abū Jaʿfar Aḥmad b. Naṣr. In this meeting, Ibn Masarra kept quiet for a long time, but when addressed by Aḥmad b. Naṣr, he answered "in an elaborate yet pleasing way" (*kalām maṣnūʿ, illā annahu ḥasan fī l-kalām jayyid*), saying: "I came to you aspiring to acquire from your light and to rely on your knowledge" (*muqtabisan min nūrika wa-mustamiddan bi-ʿilmika*) and similar things that amounted to a small *khuṭba* (Khushanī, *Ṭabaqāt*, 159–60; also Ibn ʿIdhārī, *Bayān*, 195). Even his opponents concede that he knew how to use "mellifluous speech" (*kalām ʿadhb*), though they stress the fact that he used this talent to lead people astray (Dhahabī, *Taʾrīkh*, 590, quoting Ibn al-Faraḍī), and that "using his silver tongue, he purposefully chose opaque expressions that would hide his meaning" (*wa-kāna lahu lisān yaṣilu bihi ilā taʾlīf al-kalām wa-tamwīh al-alfaẓ wa-ikhfāʾ l-maʿānī*; Ibn al-Faraḍī, *Taʾrīkh*, II, 41). But he was not a prolific writer: although his contemporary al-Khushanī says that he composed "many books," we learn from an anecdote recounted by Ibn al-Abbār that he took his time revising drafts, and was loath to part with a work before he felt it was ready (Ibn al-Abbār, *Takmila*, I, 233–34). His two extant works corroborate the impression emerging from this anecdote: they are remarkably thought out, tightly constructed, and short (Stroumsa and Sviri 2009, 213).

Notwithstanding this restrained and controlled approach to writing, our sources attribute to him several books. The number of Ibn Masarra's books remains unknown. Asín Palacios, who was aware of only two titles of Ibn Masarra's works, already assumed that he had composed more (Asín Palacios 1978, 41). A short review of what we know about Ibn Masarra's writings is in order here:

1. The Chester Beatty manuscript contains a short treatise, titled the *Epistle of Contemplation* (*Risālat al-Iʿtibār*). The attribution in the title page (*risālat al-iʿtibār li-l-faqīh Abī ʿAbd Allāh al-jabalī*) clearly identifies Ibn Masarra as its author, and the content and style of the text itself further agree with Ibn Masarra's authorship (Stroumsa and Sviri 2009, 208, 212–14, 226). The available biographical and historical sources, however, do not mention this title among Ibn Masarra's works. The treatise describes the mental practice by which a person observes the world and contemplates, in an ascending order, the different levels of existence, thus

and 214. The nature of Ibn Masarra's Neo-Platonism, and in particular the claims of his so-called Pseudo-Empedoclean teachings, deserve a separate study; see Stern 1971; De Smet 1998; Stroumsa 2002; Braun 2006. On the nature of Ibn Masarra's *bāṭinism*, and in particular his close affinity to the thought of the *Rasāʾil Ikhwān al-Ṣafāʾ*, see Tornero 1993, 63; Stroumsa and Sviri 2009, 210; and see now De Callataÿ 2014. I am grateful to Godefroid de Callataÿ for making this article available to me before publication.

proceeding to the uppermost levels of knowledge (Jaʿfar 1978; Jaʿfar 1982; Garrido Clemente 2007a; Garrido Clemente 2008; Kenny 2002; Stroumsa and Sviri 2009). Although in Ibn Masarra's discourse in this treatise one can sometimes detect echoes of Muʿtazilī theology, its overall Neoplatonic nature is unmistakable (Stroumsa and Sviri 2009).

2. The *Book of Letters*: Ibn Masarra's approach (*ṭarīqa*) to the secrets of the letters is mentioned by Ibn al-ʿArabī as one of Ibn al-ʿArabī's models for his own discourse on the subject. Ibn al-ʿArabī is careful to state his objection to preoccupation with the properties of letters, preoccupation that he also seems to associate with Ibn Masarra (*Kitāb al-Mīm*, 7). Ibn Masarra's recourse to the use of letter-speculation ("*taṣrīf Ibn Masarra fī l-ḥurūf*") is criticized also by Ibn Sabʿīn (*al-Risāla al-faqīriyya*, 14; *al-Fatḥ al-mushtarak*, 253). Ibn al-ʿArabī does not specify the source of his information regarding Ibn Masarra's approach to the secrets of letters and to their properties, nor does he associate this information with any specific book of Ibn Masarra's. Nevertheless, it stands to reason to recognize in his words a reference to the longer of the two texts discovered and published by Jaʿfar. In the Chester Beatty manuscript this work is titled *The Book of the Properties of Letters, Their True Nature and Their Origin* (*Kitāb Khawāṣṣ al-ḥurūf wa-ḥaqāʾiquhā wa-uṣūluhā*). As its name indicates, the book is dedicated to letter speculation, where the letters of the Arabic alphabet are presented as divine hypostases and as the manifestations of the divine attributes, overflowing in order to create the universe and control its destiny to eternity. The *Book of Letters* seems to present a more mature mystical-philosophical discourse than the *Epistle on Contemplation*, with clearer echoes of late-antique Neoplatonism, a difference that suggests that the *Book of Letters* was composed later (Stroumsa and Sviri 2009, 236, 239). Elsewhere, Ibn Masarra's *Book of Letters* is also explicitly mentioned by Ibn al-ʿArabī, who says that in this book, Ibn Masarra drew attention (*nabbaha*) to the meaning of the Kaʿba (*al-bayt*) and the black stone, which serves as an interpreter (*tarjumān*) between us and the different ranks of divine revelation (Ibn al-ʿArabī, *Futūḥāt*, II, 646; Massignon 1929, 31). Such a view does not appear in Ibn Masarra's *Book of Letters* as we have it, and there is no obvious saying in this book that can be regarded as a *tanbīh* to this meaning.

3. *The Book of Perspicacity* (*Kitāb al-Tabṣira*) is mentioned by Ibn al-Abbār (*Takmila*, 233–34). Relying on Muslim historiographers, Jaʿfar assumed that Ibn Masarra had written only two books (Jaʿfar 1982, 300). Having established convincingly that the text he found was named *Kitāb al-Iʿtibār*, Jaʿfar therefore proceeded to match the discovered book (bearing a previously unattested title) with an attested title (believed until then to belong to a lost work). He thus argued that the *Kitāb al-Tabṣira* mentioned by Ibn al-Abbār must have been another title of the *Kitāb al-Iʿtibār*, especially since *iʿtibār* and *istibṣār* were sometimes given a similar meaning (Jaʿfar 1982, 300–306).

Jaʿfar's identification of the two titles has been generally accepted by scholars (including myself; Strousma and Sviri 2009, 203 n. 7). But this identification deserves to be questioned. Ibn al-Abbār mentions the *Kitāb al-Tabṣira* in the context of a story about Ibn Masarra's close and devout disciple Ḥayy b. ʿAbd al-Mālik. This resident of Cordoba used to visit Ibn Masarra in his secluded place of worship in the Sierra ("*fī mutaʿabbadihi bi-l-jabal*"), where he would stay for many days each time, but then leave again. Usually, we are told, Ibn Masarra was careful to go over his own books for a whole year before revealing them. But after Ibn Masarra had completed his *Kitāb al-Tabṣira*, Ḥayy deceitfully managed to get hold of the manuscript, and to make a copy of it. To add insult to injury, this copy was not a faithful rendering of the original. After this incident, Ibn Masarra decided not to reveal his *Kitāb al-Tabṣira* to anyone (Ibn al-Abbār, *Takmila*, I, 233–34). The story (although told by the rather hostile Ibn al-Abbār) sounds credible. If so, this would mean that the *Kitāb al-Tabṣira* was never published by its author. It does not seem very likely that the work that reached us as Ibn Masarra's *Risālat al-Iʿtibār* would be a draft of *Kitāb al-Tabṣira* that Ḥayy b. ʿAbd al-Mālik published, in his master's name, despite the latter's known censorship. It is of course possible that Ibn Masarra later integrated the ideas expressed in the *Kitāb al-Tabṣira* into another book. But as mentioned above, the *Risālat al-Iʿtibār* seems to be a relatively early work of Ibn Masarra, and thus not the most likely depository for recycled material from the *Kitāb al-Tabṣira*. Be that as it may, the identification of the two books seems to be unfounded.

4. *The Book of Explanation* (*Kitāb al-Tabyīn*), is mentioned by al-Qurṭubī (d. 671/1272), who cites a prophetic tradition mentioned in it, which supports the possibility of intercession (*shafāʿa*) of the inhabitants of Paradise on behalf of the inhabitants of Hell (*Tadhkira*, 306–7; Addas 1992, 914; Brown 2006b, 42–43, 85–86). Transmitted on the authority of ʿAbd Allāh Ibn Masarra (Muḥammad's father) and of Ibn Waḍḍāḥ, the use of this *ḥadīth* by Ibn Masarra weakens the reliability of the accusations leveled against him and against his disciples that they denied intercession.

   Al-Ḥulal al-mawshiyya, which mentions another *ḥadīth* transmitted by Ibn Masarra, says that it appeared in "a compilation authored by Ibn Masarra" (*mujallad min taʾlīf Ibn Masarra*). This *ḥadīth*, about an agreement that the Prophet had made with the Jews, adds up to other pieces of information that indicate Ibn Masarra's fascination with things Jewish, as well as his preoccupation with eschatology (Stroumsa 2006; Stroumsa and Sviri 2009, 212, 228, 231, 244). Ibn Masarra's eschatological preoccupation, as well as his belief in intercession, is reflected also in another tradition attributed to Ibn Masarra, a *ḥadīth* on the intercession of ascetics (*zāhidīn*) on behalf of sinners—supposedly something that Ibn Masarra had found in the Psalter (*al-Zabūr*) (al-Thaʿālibī, *ʿUlūm*, II, 35: Morris 1973, 24; Brown 2006b, 44–45).

As mentioned above, Ibn Masarra was educated by traditional scholars like Ibn Waḍḍāḥ and al-Khushanī, and attended the circles of Mālikī jurists and *ḥadīth* scholars. Not surprisingly, his own extant works include some prophetic traditions, although he dispenses with the *isnād* (Jaʿfar 1978, 313; compare Fierro 1999, 179), and it is quite possible that in his nonextant works prophetic traditions played a more prominent role. The *Kitāb al-Tabyīn* may have been identical with the *mujallad* mentioned by *al-Ḥulal*, or it may have been another book dedicated to prophetic traditions, but it could also have been a speculative book in which a *ḥadīth* is quoted.

5. *Kitāb Tawḥīd al-mūqinīn*, to which we will return further below, is mentioned by Ibn al-Marʾa (d. 611/1214), in his *Sharḥ al-Irshād*, and the relevant lines were published by Massignon (1929, 70).
6. The *al-Muntaqā min kalām ahl al-tuqā* ("A selection from the sayings of the pious ones") is not mentioned as a work of Ibn Masarra's by any of our sources. The title page of the manuscript attributes it to a certain Aḥmad Ibn Masarra b. ʿAbd Allāh al-Qurṭubī. According to the editor of the text, Mehmet Neçmettin Bardakçi, a comparison of this text with Ibn Masarra's *Epistle of Contemplation* reinforces the likelihood that it is indeed Ibn Masarra's (Bardakçi 1998, 41–42, 132–35; Bardakçi 1999, 53). Garrido-Clemente, on the other hand (who refers to this work by the title that appears in its introduction, *al-Gharīb al-Muntaqā min kalām al-tuqā* ("A selection of extraordinary sayings from the sayings of the pious ones"), doubts Ibn Masarra's authorship and, relying on other Andalusī sources, suggests identifying the author of this book as Abū ʿAbd Allāh Ibn Khamīs al-Jābūrī (Ramón Guerrero and Garrido Clemente 2006, 150). A manuscript bearing the same title (*al-Gharīb al-Muntaqā min kalām al-tuqā*) is listed by van Koningsveld (1991:818; 1992:96, no. 33 in his list). This manuscript (Madrid, CSIC, no. 001227530), which holds indeed the same text published by Bardakçi, is presented as extracts from al-Ghazālī's *Iḥyāʾ ʿulūm al-dīn*, compiled by *al-shaykh al-faqīh* Abū al-Ḥasan ʿAlī b. ʿAbd Allāh b. Malik al-Maʿmarī al-Ubādhī. Another person involved in the compilation was a certain Aḥmad b. ʿAlī Shallūn. One should also note that the somewhat verbose style of this text (reflected in its length) seems quite different from that of the two texts published by Jaʿfar.

Apart from the book titles, some of the sources attribute to Ibn Masarra sayings that are not associated with a specific book. Al-Ḥumaydī (d. 488/1095), for example, mentions "compositions on meanings" (*tawalīf fī l-maʿānī*). These compositions may have been dedicated to the interpretation ("meaning") of Qurʾānic verses, or may have been identical with one of Ibn Masarra's known books mentioned above.

In addition to speculative thought, Ibn Masarra is said to have composed some poetry. Al-Ḥumaydī records a poem for a rainy day, in which Ibn Masarra had invited the Mālikī scholar Abū Bakr al-Luʾluʾī to join him in a place "which is indicated only by a hint, like a concealed secret" (*makān ka-l-ḍamīr al-maknī*).[4] But according to al-Ḥumaydī, this poem was recited to al-Luʾluʾī, not written in a book. Ibn al-Faraḍī cites a few lines from a poem in which Ibn Masarra lamented the death of his brother Ibrāhīm in Alexandria.[5] This poem is cited also by Ibn Ḥayyān, along with another poem by Ibn Masarra (Ibn Ḥayyān, *Muqtabas*, 32, 34). Lines from other poems are quoted by al-Kattānī (*Tashbīhāt*, 222, 271). But there is no indication that Ibn Masarra was particularly known as a poet or that his poems were collected.

All in all, we thus know of five (or six) book titles by Ibn Masarra. But there may have been more, and on the other hand, it is possible that two or more titles refer in fact to the same book. What seems certain, however, is that Ibn Masarra wrote more than the two books published by Jaʿfar.

4.2. Ibn Masarra's *Tawḥīd al-mūqinīn*

Apart from these two books, the only excerpt we have so far that is explicitly associated with a named book of Ibn Masarra's is the one cited by Ibn al-Marʾa from the *Tawḥīd al-mūqinīn*. The rest of this chapter will be devoted to this book.

Ibn al-Marʾa b. Dahhāq al-Mālaqī (d. 611/1214), a Ṣūfī author associated with "the School of Murcia," quotes Ibn Masarra's *Tawḥīd al-mūqinīn* in his commentary on al-Juwaynī's *Kitāb al-Irshād ilā qawātiʿ al-adilla fī uṣūl al-iʿtiqād* (Brown 2006b, 74). Ibn al-Marʾa's *Sharḥ al-Irshād* is still unedited, but Louis Massignon published the passage relevant to Ibn Masarra, from the Cairo manuscript, almost a century ago (Massignon 1929, 70).[6] Ibn al-Marʾa was the "*shaykh*" of Ibn Sabʿīn (d. 668/1269), or more precisely, the teacher of his teacher Ibn Aḥlā (d. 645/1247); hence Morris's observation that Ibn al-Marʾa's quotation from Ibn Masarra "witnesses to a continuous 'Ṣūfī' tradition of study of Ibn Masarra in the interval between al-Ḥumaydī and Ibn al-ʿArabī" (Morris 1973, 23; see also Brown 2006b, 82–83). The appearance of Ibn al-ʿArabī's highly sophisticated mystical system has been often regarded by scholars as unexplained, in the sense that it

[4] Ironically, this Abū Bakr al-Luʾluʾī was the teacher of the Qāḍī Muḥammad b. Yabqa b. Zarb, who was responsible later (in 350/961) for the burning of Ibn Masarra's books (Fierro 2012, 131). The invitation's wording can be either a poetic reference to Ibn Masarra's home, or it may allude already to his distant mountainous abode. Morris 1973, vi, assumes that Ibn Masarra was then still living in Cordoba, but there is no indication for it in the text, and al-Ḥumaydī cites this poem after saying that some of Cordoba's inhabitants had (already?) been led astray by him (*ʾftutina*). This poem is then quoted also by Ibn Khāqān (*Maṭmaḥ al-anfus*, 58) and al-Ḍabbī (*Bughya*, 78).

[5] Ibn al-Faraḍī, *Taʾrīkh*, I, 23; Ibn Ḥayyān, *Muqtabas*, 34. Ibn al-Faraḍī's remark that Ibrāhīm "was not like his brother" does not tell us much about either brother, but it does seem to reflect the author's animosity to Ibn Masarra.

[6] Massignon identifies the excerpt as derived from "ms. Caire, fin du t. IV, '*bāb al-malāʾika*.'" This refers in all likelihood to MS Cairo, *Dār al-Kutub al-Miṣriyya, tawḥīd* no. 6, copied in 739/1338–39. I am indebted to Jan Thiele for this information.

seems to be springing from the ground in full glory, with no apparent continuous development that gradually leads to it (ʿAfīfī 1933; Addas 1992; Sviri 1996, 78; Stroumsa and Sviri 2009, 211, 215). Morris's observation means therefore that in his view Ibn al-Marʾa's quotation from Ibn Masarra can serve as a fingerpost that may help us retrace the transmission and development of this mystical tradition. Admittedly, as a witness for such a grand tradition, this quotation is frustratingly short. Nevertheless, if we collate it with other, in themselves equally meager pieces of evidence, it may allow us to add some missing pieces to Ibn Masarra's still largely incomplete puzzle.

The book's title, *God's Unity as Upheld by Those Who Know with Certainty*, (*Tawḥīd al-mūqinīn*) tallies with what we know from other sources regarding Ibn Masarra's thought.

The preoccupation with the meaning of *tawḥīd* is of course inherent to Muslim thought. Divine attributes seem to have taken a prominent place in Ibn Masarra's unitarian thought, as they did in the thought of the followers of the Muʿtazila, "the proponents of Divine Unity and Justice" (*ahl al-ʿadl wa-l-tawḥīd*). This, however, is not sufficient to warrant seeing the origins of Ibn Masarra's thought in early Muʿazilī discussions (compare Morris 1973, 23; Arnaldez 1986, 868. Ramón Guerrero and Garrido Clemente 2006, 150).

Significantly, Ibn Masarra does not seem to be concerned with the meaning of *īmān* ("belief") or of *islām*, two equally central concepts, germane to the issue of *tawḥīd.* Discussions of these two concepts were often of legal character, as they served to delineate the community of believers, in an attempt to draw a clear line between it and those outside, both heretics and infidels (Stroumsa 1999, 1–7). A question regarding the typical traits of the believer (*ṣifat al-muʾmin*), addressed to "one of the ascetics (*baʿḍ al-zuhhād*)," is attributed to Dhū l-Nūn al-Miṣrī, who may have been one of Ibn Masarra's sources of inspiration (Ibn al-Khayr, *Fahrasa*, 274). Several historiographical sources accuse Ibn Masarra as well as the so-called Masarrīs of distancing themselves from the rest of the Muslim community. Ibn Masarra is said "to have adopted an aloof comportment" (*maʿrūf bi-madhhab min al-iʿtizāl*—Abū l-Walīd Ibn al-Faraḍī, quoted in *Muqtabas*, 32; "*inqabaḍa ʿan akthar al-nās*"—al-Khushanī, *Akhbār*, 135), and the Masarrīs are similarly accused of advocating separation from the community (*qālū bi-l-iʿtizāl ʿan al-ʿāmma*), of neglecting to properly salute their fellow Muslims, and of regarding non-Masarrīs as outside the pale of Islam. In both cases, the wording of the accusation may well be intended also to derisively insinuate their supposed Muʿtazilī inclinations (although, as mentioned above, Ibn Masarra was not a Muʿtazilī, nor were his followers, and, in general, the Muʿtazila as a movement did not get a foothold in Andalus [see Stroumsa 2014]). But the main thrust of the accusation is clearly a condemnation of their social alienation. It has been suggested that, in the case of the Masarrīs (and especially Ismāʿīl al-Ruʿaynī and the circle of his followers), this antisocial behavior may have reflected their doubts regarding the religious state of those outside their circle; if the belief of the others is faulty, and they are not true Muslims, then withdrawal from their midst would be a religious obligation, as would the refusal to salute them as Muslims (*Muqtabas*, 20–24, 30–36; Brown 2006b, 50–51; Morris 1973, 35). According to Ibn Ḥazm, Ismāʿīl al-Ruʿaynī considered al-Andalus to be *dār kufr*, and went so far as to declare licit the killing of those who did not follow him (Ibn Ḥazm, *Fiṣal*, V, 67; repeated in al-ʿAsqalānī, *Lisān al-mīzān*, I, 466). Whether or not this line of thought dictated the behavior of al-Ruʿaynī's followers, nothing in Ibn Masarra's writings suggests such preoccupation with the predominantly legal definition of who is a believer. His interest in the meaning of *tawḥīd*, philosophical and theological in character, goes in completely different directions, and his *iʿtizāl* was most probably also not a result of such legal concern, but of the search for the seclusion required for mystical contemplation.

Closely related to the issue of divine unity is the epistemological quest for unequivocal knowledge (*yaqīn*). Both the *Risālat al-Iʿtibār* and the *Kitāb al-Ḥurūf* present ways to achieve this knowledge, the first through the correct contemplative practice, the object of which is the physical world, the second through deciphering the ontological significance of the Arabic letters. At the outset of the *Epistle of Contemplation* Ibn Masarra states:

> [God] sent the prophets, God's prayers and blessings upon them, to proclaim to people and to clarify for them the esoteric things, and to attest to these things by manifest signs. This is in order that they may attain certitude (*yaqīn*), for which they will be recompensed and brought to account, and on which they will be questioned. (Jaʿfar 1978, 350; Stroumsa and Sviri 2009, 217)

The success or failure in the quest for certitude, perceived as essential for human salvation, thus has grave soteriological consequences. The success in this quest is described as the attainment of human perfection, when, at the end of the contemplative process, "certitude is revealed, and the hearts attain the realities of faith" (Jaʿfar 1978, 351; Stroumsa and Sviri 2009, 218). During a human life, the pursuit of certitude is an ever-continuing process:

> The more the contemplator observes, the more he sees, and the more he sees, the stronger he becomes in conviction (*taṣdīq*), divine aid (*tawfīq*), certitude (*yaqīn*) and beholding (*istibṣār*). (Jaʿfar 1978, 359; Stroumsa and Sviri 2009, 225)

The end result of this process is the attainment of "the knowledge of the Book," and with it, the aspired to rank of the *mūqinūn*:

> No mortal can attain knowledge of the science of the Book unless he brings together what is recounted with contemplation, and verifies that which he hears by that which he beholds. May God include us and you among those who have certitude, those who seek to behold (*min al-mūqinīn al-mustabṣirīn*). (Jaʿfar 1978, 351; Stroumsa and Sviri 2009, 219)

Although the concept *yaqīn* is more prominent in the *Epistle of Contemplation*, which is wholly dedicated to the quest for knowing and understanding, its significance is also clearly stated in the *Book of Letters*. In the beginning of the book Ibn Masarra describes the three complexes (*jumal*), which together make up the entire, all-encompassing science contained in God's revealed book. Ibn Masarra characterizes each of these three complexes by the instruments and practices typical to it and which are its epistemological tools, as well as by its ultimate epistemological outcome. The first and highest complex, the science of Lordship (*ʿilm al-rubūbiyya*), is characterized by "its indications (*dalāʾil*) and attestations (*shawāhid*)," as well as by its outcome, which is the unequivocal, certain knowledge (*yaqīn*; Jaʿfar 1978, 312).

The title *Tawḥīd al-mūqinīn* thus suggests that, unlike the two other extant books, which dealt with the process of attaining knowledge of the truth, either through contemplation of the world or by uncovering the revelation crafted in letters, this third book was focused on the truth itself, in its purest form. The analysis of this bold title indicates that the book dealt with the core of Ibn Masarra's mystical philosophy, namely his perception of the divine as it becomes known to the happy few who know with certitude.

In this sense, the *mūqinūn* are clearly an elite group. As mentioned above, the Masarrīs were accused of denying prophetic intercession, and of claiming the possibility to attain prophecy. In the case of Ibn Masarra himself, as we have seen, the transmission of prophetic traditions attributed to him suggests on the contrary that intercession played some role in his thought. But the accusations against him and his followers can reflect either the Masarrīs' aspiration for direct contact with the divine truth (an aspiration that is clearly discernible in the thought of Ibn Masarra himself), or the way this aspiration was interpreted by others.

In addition to the name of the book, Ibn al-Marʾa's reference to Ibn Masarra also presents its content (or at least, one of the ideas it contained). The text reads as follows:[7]

> Ibn Masarra said in his book *Tawḥīd al-mūqinīn* that the attributes of God, the Blessed, are infinite in number. According to him,[8] God's knowledge is living,[9] knowing, powerful, hearing, seeing, and speaking. In the same way, His power is described as living, knowing, powerful, willing, and having a hearing with which it hears. The same applies to all His attributes. He said: "This is the way to proclaim God's unity."[10] He thus depicted the attributes as Gods. This is also what he said regarding the attributes of the attributes,[11] *ad infinitum*. He thus made God into an infinite number of gods—may we find refuge in God.

It is not clear what part, if any, of this text is an exact quotation of Ibn Masarra's own words and how much of it is a paraphrase. As Ibn al-Marʾa is clearly opposed to

7 قال ابن مسرة في كتابه توحيد الموقنين بان صفات الله سبحانه لا نهاية لعددها فعلم الله عنده حي عالم قادر سامع بصير متكلم وكذلك قدرته موصوفة بانها حية عالمة قادرة مريدة لها سمع تسمع به وكذلك القول في جميع صفاته وقال هكذا هو التوحيد فقد صير الصفات الهة وكذلك قوله في صفات الصفات الى غير نهاية فجعل الاله الهة لا نهاية لها, والعياذ بالله.

8 Brown 2006b, 74, reads "*ʿindihi*" and translates "with respect to Him."

9 Brown 2006b, 74, translates "a Living One" etc.

10 "*Hākadhā huwa l-tawḥīd*." I understand *tawḥīd* here as a human action. Compare Brown 2006b, 74: "this is divine unity."

11 Brown 2006b, 74, apparently regards the "attribute of attributes" as a redundancy due to a copyist's error, and corrects it in his translation.

Ibn Masarra's position, it is also evident that his presentation distorts Ibn Masarra's ideas. His interpretation of Ibn Masarra's position is a hostile caricature, whereby Ibn Masarra's theory of attributes makes him a polytheist, whereas for Ibn Masarra himself the theory of attributes was part of his attempt to preserve God's unity to the utmost. Ibn al al-Marʾa's presentation also implies that Ibn Masarra accepted the validity of an actual infinite series as well as the possibility of one attribute being also the attribute of another attribute. Both claims would be considered serious breaches of commonly held scientific axioms: actual infinite series were rejected by practically everyone; and the *mutakallimūn*'s atomism precluded the possibility of one accident residing in another.

Nevertheless, if we ignore Ibn al-Marʾa's hostile interpretation, this text does agree with what other sources tell us about Ibn Masarra's position regarding the attributes. Although only a few lines long, this text summarizes what proclaiming God's unity—and we may add, proclaiming God's unity, as do those who have certitude—means. Correct understanding of the divine attributes lies at the heart of this true *tawḥīd*. The statement quoted by Ibn al-Marʾa indicates precisely that for Ibn Masarra the divine attributes are not accidents. On the other hand, we can assume that, in the terminology of the general debate over the attributes, Ibn Masarra would probably say that the attributes are also not entities (*maʿānī*) and have no separate, independent ontological value. Although human beings use the same wording—knowing, powerful, willing, and so on—to describe human attributes, the interchangeability of the divine attributes and the way they flow into one another in Ibn al-Marʾa's presentation distinguish them from the ontological distinctiveness, the plurality, and the corporeality of human attributes.

Scriptural language dictates the use of these attributes, but in Ibn Masarra's thought the Qurʾānic terminology—the divine attributes and God's ninety-nine beautiful names—becomes steps in the ladder leading up to the knowledge of the one God, a ladder that presumably, once this knowledge is attained, is no longer necessary. The imagery of the ladder of ascension appears explicitly in both of Ibn Masarra's extant works. In the *Epistle of Contemplation* Ibn Masarra presents the world, with all its creatures and signs, as a ladder by which those who contemplate ascend to the great signs of God on high (Stroumsa and Sviri 2009, 218, 230; and see Altmann 1967). In the *Book of Letters* he cites the prophetic tradition that says: "On the day of resurrection the reciter of the Qurʾān will be told: 'Recite and ascend, for you are at the last step,' " and adds: "The number of the levels of Paradise is equal to the number of the verses in the Qurʾān, which is equal to the number of the names" (Jaʿfar 1978, 313). In this context, it is interesting to note the saying attributed by Ibn al-Farrāḍ to the Sālimiyya, to whose circle Ibn Masarra may have become close during his Meccan sojourn. According to this saying, "Through a single attribute God comprehends that which He comprehends through all His attributes" (Brown 2006b, 42 and n. 92; Böwering 1979, 94).

Ibn Masarra's position on the attributes as presented here is strikingly similar to the one ascribed by Ibn Ṣāʿid al-Andalusī to the Greek philosopher Empedocles. Ibn Ṣāʿid interrupts his discussion of Empedocles in order to note that "Muḥammad b. ʿAbd Allāh

Ibn Masarra *al-jabalī al-bāṭinī* of Cordoba was a fervent follower of [Empedocles's] philosophy, steadily striving to study it." He then says:

> Empedocles was the first whose approach combined the meanings of God's attributes (*maʿānī ṣifāt Allāh*), saying that they all come down to one thing, and that, although He is described by [the terms] "knowledge," "benevolence," and "power," He does not possess distinct entities (*maʿānin*)[12] which are characterized specifically by these diverse names. Rather, He is the truly One, who has no plurality in any way whatsoever, as opposed to other beings. For [all] the "ones" in this world are subject to plurality, either in their parts or in their entities, or in that they have parallels. But the essence of the Creator is above all this.

Ibn Ṣāʿid concludes this passage by stating that, regarding the divine attributes, this was also the approach of Abū l-Hudhayl al-ʿAllāf al-Baṣrī (Ibn Ṣāʿid, *Ṭabaqāt*, 73; repeated in Ibn Abī Uṣaybiʿa, *ʿUyūn*, 37).

This passage in Ibn Ṣāʿid's *Ṭabaqāt al-umam*, which seems to associate Ibn Masarra with both Empedocles and Abū l-Hudhayl, is largely responsible for the emergence of two enduring theories in the history of modern scholarship of Andalusī philosophy: that of the so-called Pseudo-Empedocles (associated by Asín Palacios with "the school of Ibn Masarra"), and that of the Andalusī Muʿtazilī school. The discussion of these two theories, both equally unfounded and yet, phantom-like, quite persistent, is beyond the scope of this chapter (see van-Ess 1991–97, 4:272–74; Tornero 1985; De-Smet 1998; Stroumsa 2002; Brown 2006b, 94–103; Stroumsa 2014). In the present context, Ibn Ṣāʿid's information is important only insofar as he too sees Ibn Masarra's approach to the attributes as reflecting a strict theology of unity (Morris 1973, 37).

In the same vein, Ibn Ḥazm of Cordoba reports that Ibn Masarra used to say that God's knowledge and His power are both temporal, created attributes (*ṣifatāni muḥdathatāni makhlūqatāni*), and that God has two [kinds of] knowledge, both of them temporal: the first is God's knowledge of universals (*kulliyyāt*; or, in another version, His knowledge of the Book), which is the knowledge of that which is hidden (*ʿilm al-ghayb*), and His knowledge of the particulars and of that which is seen (*ʿilm al-shahāda*). For Ibn Ḥazm, this distinction proved Ibn Masarra's agreement with the Muʿtazila regarding free will (*qadar*), since it allowed Ibn Masarra to preserve God's omniscience while allowing for human exercise of free will (Ibn Ḥazm, *Fiṣal*, V, 65–66). The use of the Qurʾānic vocabulary in Ibn Ḥazm's report fits indeed Ibn Masarra's thought, as we know it from his *Book of Letters*, where Ibn Masarra says:

> Therefore He, greater than any speaker, said: "He knows the hidden and the manifest" (Qurʾān 13:9). For all things are two things: external and inner. He possesses

[12] The use of the word "entities" (*maʿānin*) to denote the ontological reality of the attributes is well attested. Nevertheless, and despite Ibn Masarra's apparently well-known interest in this topic, it does not seem likely that in al-Ḥumaydī's above-mentioned reference to Ibn Masarra's "compositions on the *maʿānī*" he intended compositions devoted specifically to this subject.

> the knowledge, which encompasses the inner and the external. The [knowledge] encompassing the inner is unique to Him. It is His preserved tablet and His concealed name, that is, *Lām*. And the [knowledge] encompassing the external, namely the body of the whole, is the greater soul. This is the dominion (*mulk*), and it is what He, of exalted memory, referred to by *Mīm*. (Jaʿfar 1978, 326)

Further on, Ibn Masarra returns to these two kinds of knowledge and says:

> From the first attribute, which pertains to the letter *ṣād*, God is named maker (*ṣāniʿ*) and creator, a form-giver (*muṣawwir*); by it He made all. . . . Explaining the first attribute, God said: "He is God, there is no God but He, the knower of the hidden and the manifest, He is the merciful, the compassionate." (Qurʾān 59:22; Jaʿfar 1978, 329)

And he returns to the combination of "the hidden and manifest knowledge" yet again, saying:

> The knowledge of the hidden is the primordial one, and the knowledge of the manifest is the lower knowledge which encompasses the completed existents, those existents that left the domain of the possible and appeared, becoming manifest to sight. Therefore God said: "He knows the hidden and the manifest." (Jaʿfar 1978, 339)

Ibn Ḥazm's report thus seems to rely on close familiarity with Ibn Masarra's sayings. In Ibn Masarra's thought, the distinction between two kinds of divine knowledge served to explain God's involvement in the world—its creation and the knowledge of the existent beings—while preserving His detachment from the changing and multiple beings. By presenting the two facets of the attribute of knowing, Ibn Masarra manages to keep the complete unity of God, the Creator. Ibn Ḥazm clearly misinterprets Ibn Masarra's ideas when he attributes to him the saying that "God's knowledge is other than God" (*Fiṣal*, II, 128–29). Nevertheless, behind Ibn Ḥazm's misrepresentation we can recognize again, on the one hand the notoriety of Ibn Masarra's preoccupation with divine attributes, and on the other hand Ibn Masarra's attempt to reach, beyond the attributes, to the completely transcendental One.

Ibn Masarra's preoccupation with divine attributes may have been fed by *kalām* discussions, and Ibn Ṣāʿid is probably right in presenting Ibn Masarra's ideas as closer to the formulations adopted by the Muʿtazila then to traditionalist positions. Nevertheless, Ibn Masarra is not driven by Muʿtazilī concerns, but rather thinking of the Qurʾānic text in the context of a mystical emanation theology. Ibn Ṣāʿid's association of Ibn Masarra in this context with Abū l-Hudhayl al-ʿAllāf says more about Ibn Ṣāʿid's knowledge of the Muʿtazila than about Ibn Masarra's association with them.

4.2.1. Throne

The paragraph in Ibn al-Marʾa presents the theological, rational side of Ibn Masarra's thought. Its treatment of the divine attributes stresses the unparalleled and wholly transcendental nature of God's unity, while maintaining the scriptural language and what it says about God's relation to the world. If this were our only source of information regarding Ibn Masarra, we could have come to the conclusion that it presents a full picture of Ibn Masarra's position, but the opinion we would have formed of him in that case would have been quite wrong. In line with his Neoplatonic, mystical thought, Ibn Masarra's discussion of the divine attributes also has a figurative, mythical side. The divine Throne plays an important role in his thought, and, although it is not mentioned by Ibn al-Marʾa, it is relevant to our discussion here.

The Throne (*ʿarsh*) appears several times in Ibn Masarra's extant writings. In the *Epistle of Contemplation* it is the first created being, and it encompasses all things. The Throne is identified with the universal intellect (*ʿaql*), and within it God "inscribed all His decrees and rulings and that upon which His will is borne" (Stroumsa and Sviri 2009; 224, 237). In the *Book of Letters* the Throne is identified with the Tablet (*al-lawḥ*) and with the letter *Lām*. Ibn Masarra also mentions briefly the four angels who carry the Throne, but he does not describe them in detail (Jaʿfar 1978, 332, 333, 334, 336, and 340).

A more detailed description of these four angels appears in Ibn al-ʿArabī's *Meccan Revelations*, where Ibn al-ʿArabī states that, according to what was transmitted from (*ruwīnā ʿan*) Ibn Masarra, the Throne, which is carried by the angels, is kingship or sovereignty (*mulk*). It is constrained by a body, spirit, sustenance, and rank ("*wa-huwa maḥṣūr fī jism wa-rūḥ wa-ghidhāʾ wa-martaba*"). He further says that Ādam and Isrāfīl are in charge of the forms (*li-l-ṣuwar*); Jībrīl and Muḥammad in charge of the spirits; Mīkāʾīl and Ibrāhīm in charge of livelihoods ("*arzāq*") and sustenance (*ghidhāʾ*); and Mālik and Riḍwān in charge of the promise and threat. At the end of the same chapter, Ibn al-ʿArabī mentions Ibn Masarra again in connection with the form of the Throne's four carriers: one of these angels, he says, is in the form of a man, the second in the form of a lion, the third in the form of an eagle, and the fourth in the form of a bull (Ibn al-ʿArabī, *Futūḥāt*, 348, 355; Stroumsa 2006, 103–4). The ultimate dependence of this description on the book of Ezekiel and on Jewish speculations on the divine Chariot is obvious (see Asín Palacios 1978, 77 and n. 13, who cites Munk 1859, 492). The question remains, who introduced this detailed description: Ibn al-ʿArabī himself, or Ibn Masarra.

The description of the Throne's carriers does not appear in the two texts published by Jaʿfar, and indeed Ibn al-ʿArabī does not say where he found this information (compare Tornero 1993, 60, who understood Ibn al-ʿArabī as referring to the *Book of Letters*; and see Stroumsa 2006, 103). The attribution to Ibn Masarra of a statement according to which the archangel Mīkāʾīl and the prophet Ibrāhīm are in charge of livelihoods ("*arzāq*") is repeated elsewhere by Ibn al-ʿArabī (*Fuṣūṣ*, 69; Morris 1973, 23–24), which is why I am inclined to believe that Ibn al-ʿArabī indeed took the chariot-image from Ibn Masarra.

What we hear about Ibn Masarra's supposed disciples strengthens this possibility. One of Ismāʿīl al-Ruʿaynī's "seven theses" (*aqwāl sabʿa*) was "that the Throne governs the world" (*inna l-ʿarsh huwa lladhī yudabbiru l-ālam*; Ibn Ḥazm, *Fiṣal*, IV, 199–200; Asín, pp. 106–117m counts, in fact, eight theses).). Ibn Ḥazm relates this information on the authority of al-Ruʿaynī's grandson, but adds that al-Ruʿaynī's own son denied his nephew's information (Ibn Ḥazm, *Fiṣal*, IV, 138, V, 65–67; al-ʿAsqalānī, *Lisān al-mīzān*, I, 466). For al-Ruʿaynī, this "thesis" seems to have been followed necessarily from God's complete transcendence, for "God is above having any act attributed to him" (*inna llāh ajall min an yūṣafa bi-an yafʿala shaʾyan qatt*; Ibn Ḥazm, *Fiṣal*, IV, 138, V, 65–67; al-ʿAsqalānī, *Lisān al-mīzān*, I, 466).[13] Following Ibn Ḥazm, Morris regards the attribution of this idea to Ibn Masarra as doubtful (Morris 1973, 31–32). But Ibn Masarra's own texts suggest that there was a strong basis for the association of these sayings regarding the Throne with Ibn Masarra, by both al-Ruʿaynī and Ibn al-ʿArabī. They may have found these sayings in Ibn Masarra's oral teaching, as Morris (26 n. 37) suggests, or in another yet unknown text of Ibn Masarra's. Ibn al-ʿArabī's words: "*ruwīnā ʿan* . . ." could point to oral transmission. Alternatively, it can indicate that the description of the divine Chariot, or part of this description, may have appeared in one of Ibn Masarra's collections (*tawālīf*) containing prophetic traditions. Since, however, this description relates to God's governance of the world and touches on the more esoteric aspects of *tawḥīd*, it is also quite possible (and to my mind, a more likely possibility), that the description of the Throne was also part of the *Tawḥīd al-mūqinīn*.

As mentioned above, the publication of Ibn Masarra's texts by Jaʿfar categorically disproved some suggestions regarding Ibn Masarra's thought that had been put forward by eminent scholars on the basis of excerpts in later sources. This can serve as a reminder, if a reminder is required, of how careful one must be in relying on later sources, and in particular in reconstructing from them the missing pieces (and see Schwarz 1972). And yet, bearing this caveat in mind, we must do with whatever material we possess. The present attempt to squeeze more information from the few lines in Ibn al-Marʾa's *Sharḥ al-Irshād* is such a speculative reconstruction, which relies on the agreement between this short text and other sources. It is hoped that this chapter may be of help in discovering other texts of Ibn Masarra, and that these texts, in turn, will prove, disprove, or correct the suggestions brought here.

Acknowledgments

My warm thanks go to Sabine Schmidtke and to Godefroid de Callataÿ for their insightful comments on a draft of this chapter, and to Maribel Fierro for her kind help. I further wish to thank James Morris and Vahid Brown for generously allowing me access to their unpublished work (two very impressive seminar papers, both *coups de maître*, which remain indispensable for the study of Ibn Masarra's work). I am grateful to Kadir Gombeyaz for his assistance in getting access to Bardakçi's doctoral thesis and for his

[13] Also relevant here is the place of the Throne in the thought of Dhū l-Nūn al-Ikhmīmī (d. 330/941); on this, and on its possible influence on Ibn Masarra, see Makki 1968, 155–62. On Ibn Masarra's possible connection to the thought of Dhū l-Nūn as well al-Nahrajūrī's, see Ibn al-Faraḍī, *Taʾrīkh*, 323–24.

help in clarifying the authorship of *al-Muntaqā*. I also wish to thank the library team of the Wissenschaftskolleg zu Berlin for their help in procuring a copy of Bardakçi's book.

References

Addas, C. 1992. "Andalusī Mysticism and the Rise of Ibn ʿArabī." In *The Legacy of Muslim Spain*, vol. 2, ed. S. K. Jayyusi. Leiden: Brill. 909–33.

ʿAfīfī, Abū'l-ʿAlā. 1933. "*Min ayna shtaqā Muḥyī al-Dīn b. al-ʿArabī falsafatahu al-ṣūfiyya?*" *Al-Jāmiʿa al-Miṣriyya, Majallat kuliyyat al-ādāb* 1.1: 3–45.

Altmann, A. 1967. "The Ladder of Ascension." In *Studies in Mysticism and Religion Presented to Gershom G. Scholem*. Jerusalem: Magnes, 1–32. Reprinted in A. Altmann, *Studies in Religious Philosophy and Mysticism*. Ithaca, NY: Cornell University Press, 1969, 41–72.

Arberry, A. J. 1955–66. *The Chester Beatty Library: A Handlist of the Arabic Manuscripts*. Dublin: Emery Walker.

Asín Palacios, M. 1978. *The Mystical Philosophy of Ibn Masarra and His Followers*. Trans. E. H. Douglas and H. W. Yoder. Leiden: Brill, 1978. Originally published as *Abenmasarra y su escuela: Orígenes de la filosofía hispano-musulmana* (Madrid: Imprenta Ibérica, 1914).

Bardakçi, Neçmettin Mehmet. 1998. *Ebu Abdullah Muhammed Ibn Meserre'nin tasavvufî düsünce tarihindeki yeri ve "El-Münteka mîn Kelâm Ehli't-Tükâ" Adli Eseri 73277*. Isparta: Süleyman Demirel University.

Bardakçi, Neçmettin Mehmet, trans. 1999. İbn Meserre, *El-Münteka Muttakilerin Yolu*. Istanbul: Insan yayinlari.

Böwering, G. 1979. *The Mystical Vision of Existence in Classical Islam: The Qur'anic Hermeneutics of the Sufi Sahl At-Tustari (d.283/896)*. New York: De Gruyter.

Brown, Vahid J. 2006a. "Andalusī Mysticism: A Recontextualization." *Journal of Islamic Philosophy* (Ann Arbor, MI) 2: 69–101.

Brown, Vahid J. 2006b. "Muḥammad b. Masarra al-Jabalī and His Place in Medieval Islamicate Intellectual History: Towards a Reappraisal." Reed College. Unpublished.

Cruz Hernández, M. 1981. "La persecución anti-masarrī durante el reinado de ʿAbd al-Raḥmān al-Nāṣir li-dīn Allāh segun Ibn Ḥayyān." *Al-Qanṭara* 2: 51–67; corrections in *Al-Qanṭara* 3 (1986): 482–83.

Cruz Hernández, M. 1996. *Historia del pensamiento en el mundo islámico* Vol 2: *El pensamiento de al-Andalus (siglos IX–XIV)*. Madrid: Alianza Editorial.

Ḍabbī, al-. (*Bughya*). 1884. *Bughyat al-Multamis fī ta'rīkh rijāl ahl al-Andalus*. Ed. F. Codera and J. Ribera. Madrid.

De Callataÿ, G. 2014. "Philosophy and Bāṭinism in al-Andalus: Ibn Masarra's *Risālat al-iʿtibār* and the *Rasā'il Ikhwān al-Ṣafā'*." *Jerusalem Studies in Arabic and Islam* 41:261-312.

De Smet, D. 1998. *Empedocles Arabus: Une lecture néoplatonicienne tardive*. Brussels: Koninklijke Academie voor Wetenschappen, Letteren en Schone Kunsten; Turnhout: Brepols.

Ebstein, M., and S. Sviri. 2011. "The So-Called *Risālat al-ḥurūf* (Epistle on Letters) Ascribed to Sahl al-Tustarī and Letter Mysticism in al-Andalus." *Journal Asiatique* 299: 213–70.

Fierro, M. 1999. "Opposition to Sufism in al-Andlaus." In *Islamic Mysticism Contested: Thirteen Centuries of Controversies and Polemics*, ed. F. De Jong and B. Radtke. Leiden: Brill, 174–206.

Fierro, M. 2012. "Plants, Mary the Copt, Abraham, Donkeys and Knowledge: Again on Bāṭinism during the Umayyad Caliphate in al-Andalus." In *Differenz und Dynamik im*

Islam. Festschrift für Heinz Halm zum 70. Geburtstag, ed. H. H. Biesterfeldt and V. Klemm. Würzburg: Ergon, 125–44.

Garrido Clemente, P. 2007a. "Edición crítica de la *Risālat al-Iʿtibār* de Ibn Masarra de Córdoba." *Miscelánea de Estudios Árabes y Hebraicos, Sección Árabe-Islam* 56: 81–104.

Garrido Clemente, P. 2007b. "Edición crítica del *K. Jawāṣṣ al-ḥurūf* de Ibn Masarra." *Al-Andalus-Magreb* 14: 51–89.

Garrido Clemente, P. 2008. "Traducción anotada de la *Risālat al-Iʿtibār* de Ibn Masarra de Córdoba." *Estudios humanisticos, Filología* 30: 139–63.

Al-Ḥulal al-mawshiyya fī dhikri al-akhbār al-marrākushiyya (*Ḥulal*). N.d. Ed. al-Bashīr al-Fūrati. Tunis: Maṭbaʿat al-taqaddum al-islāmiyya.

Ḥumaydī, Abū ʿAbd Allāh Muḥammad b. Abī Naṣr b. Fattūḥ al-. (*Jadhwa*) 1952. *Jadhwat al-muqtabas fī dhikri wulāt al-Andalus*. Ed. al-Ṭanjī. Cairo: *Maktabat al-thaqāfa al-islāmiyya*.

Ibn al-Abbār, Abū ʿAbd Allāh Muḥammad b. ʿAbd Allāh. (*Takmila*) 1995. *Al-Takmila li-Kitāb al-Ṣila*. Ed. ʿAbd al-Salām al-Harās. Beirut: Dār al-Fikr.

Ibn al-ʿArabī, Muḥyī al-Dīn Abū ʿAbd Allāh Muḥammad b. ʿAlī. (*Fuṣūṣ*) 2003. *Fuṣūṣ al-ḥikam*, Ed. ʿA. I. al-Kayyālī and al-Ḥusaynī al-Shādhilī al-Darkāwī. Beirut: Dār al-kutub al-ʿilmiyya.

Ibn al-ʿArabī. (*Futūḥāt*) 1972. *Al-Futūḥāt al-Makiyya*. Ed. ʿUthmān Yaḥyā and Ibrāhīm Madkūr. Cairo: al-Hayʾa al-Miṣriyya al-ʿāmma liʾl-kitāb.

Ibn al-ʿArabī. (*Kitāb al-Mīm*) 2002. *Kitāb al-Mīm waʾl-Wāw waʾl-Nūn*. Ed. C.-A. Gilis. Beirut: Albouraq.

Ibn al-Faraḍī. (*Taʾrīkh*) 1954. *Taʾrīkh al-ʿulamāʾ waʾl-ruwāt liʾl-ʿilm*. Ed. ʿIzzat al-Aṭṭār al-Ḥusaynī. Cairo: Maktabat al-Khānjī.

Ibn Ḥayyān. (*Muqtabas*) 1979. *Al-Muqtabas*. Vol. 5. Ed. P. Chalmeta. Madrid.

Ibn ʿIdhārī. (*Bayān*) 1948. *Al-Bayān al-mughrib fī akhbār al-Andalus wa-l-Maghrib*. Ed. G. S. Kolan and E. Lévi-Provençal. Leiden: Brill.

Ibn al-Khair al-Ishbīlī, Abū Bakr Muḥammad b. ʿUmar. 1893. *Fahrasat mā rawāhu min shuyūkhihi min al-dawāwīn al-muṣannafa fī ḍurūb al-ʿilm wa-anwāʿ al-maʿārif*. Ed. Franciscus Codera and J. Ribera Tarrago. 2 vols. Saragossa: BAH, vol. ix–x

Ibn Khāqān. (*Maṭmaḥ al-anfus*) 1302/1884–85. *Maṭmaḥ al-anfus wa-masraḥ al-taʾannus fi mulaḥ ahl al-āndalus*. Istanbul: Maṭbaʿat al-Jawāʾib.

Ibn Sabʿīn. (*al-Fatḥ al-Mushtarak*). 1965. *Al-Fatḥ al-Mushtarak*. In *Rasāʾil Ibn Sabʿīn*, ed. ʿAbd al-Raḥmān Badawī. Cairo: Al-Muʾassasa al-miṣriyya al-ʿāmma li-l-taʾlīf wa-anbāʾ wa-l-nashr.

Ibn Sabʿīn. (*al-Risāla al-faqīriyya*). *Al-Risāla al-faqīriyya*. In *Rasāʾil Ibn Sabʿīn*, ed. ʿAbd al-Raḥmān Badawī. Cairo: Al-Muʾassasa al-miṣriyya al-ʿāmma li-l-taʾlīf wa-anbāʾ wa-l-nashr.

Ibn Ṣāʿid. (*Ṭabaqāt al-umam*) 1985. *Ṭabaqāt al-umam*. Ed. Ḥ. Bū ʿAlwān. Beirut: Dār al-ṭalīʿa.

Jaʿfar, Muḥammad Kamāl Ibrāhīm. 1978. *Min qaḍāyā al-fikr al-islāmī*. Cairo: Maktabat Dār al-ʿulūm.

Jaʿfar, Muḥammad Kamāl Ibrāhīm. 1982. *Min al-turāth al-falsafi: Ibn Masarra, taḥqīq wa-taḥlīl wa-naqḍ*. Cairo: al-Majlis al-aʿlā li-l-thaqāfa.

al-Kattānī, Abū ʿAbd Allāh Muḥammad b. al-Kattānī al-Ṭabīb. (*Tashbīhāt*) N.d. *Kitāb al-Tashbīhāt min ashʿār ahl Andalus*. Ed. Iḥsān ʿAbbās. Beirut: Dār al-thaqāfa.

Kenny, J. 2002. "Ibn-Masarra: His *Risāla al-iʿtibār*." *Orita: Ibadan Journal of Religious Studies* 34: 1–26.

Al-Khushanī, Abū ʿAbd Allāh Muḥammad b. Ḥārith (*Akhbār*). N.d. *Akhbār al-fuqahāʾ wa-l-muḥaddithīn*. Ed. Sālim Muṣṭafā al-Badrī. Beirut: Dār al-kutub al-ʿilmiyya.

Al-Khushanī, Abū ʿAbd Allāh Muḥammad b. al-Ḥārith b. Asad. (*Ṭabaqāt*) 1914. *Kitāb Ṭabaqāt ʿulamāʾ ifriqiyya*. Ed. Mohammed ben Cheneb. Alger: Bastide Jourdain.

Makki, M. A. 1968. *Ensayo sobre las aportaciones orientales en la España musulmana y su influencia en la formación de la cultura hispano-árabe*. Madrid: Instituto de Estudios Islámicos.

Massignon, L. 1929. *Recueil de textes inédits concernant l'histoire de la mystique en pays d'Islam*. Paris: Paul Geuthner.

Morris, J. W. 1973. *Ibn Masarra: A Reconsideration of the Primary Sources*. Harvard University [unpublished manuscript, available for download at http://hdl.handle.net/2345/4254]

Munk, S. 1859. *Mélanges de philosophie juive et arabe*. Paris: A. Franck.

Qurṭubī. (*al-ʿUlūm al-fākhira*) 1317/1899–1900. *Al-ʿUlūm al-fākhira fī l-naẓar fī l-umūr al-ākhira*. Cairo.

Ramón Guerrero, R., and P. Garrido Clemente. 2006. "Ibn Masarra al-Qurṭubī." In *Biblioteca de al-Andalus*, vol. 4: Almería, *Enciclopedia de la Cultura Andalusí*, ed. J. Lirola Delgado, no. 788, 144–54.

Safran, J. M. 2013. *Defining Boundaries in al-Andalus: Muslims, Christians and Jews in Islamic Iberia*. Ithaca, NY: Cornell University Press.

Schwarz, M. 1971. "Can We Rely on Later Authorities for the Views of Earlier Thinkers?" *Israel Oriental Studies* 2: 241–48.

Stern, S. M. 1971. "Ibn Masarra, Follower of Pseudo-Empedocles—an Illusion." In *Actas IV Congresso de estudos árabes e islâmicos. Coimbra–Lisboa. 1 a 8 de Setembro de 1968*. Leiden: Brill, 325–37.

Stroumsa, S. 1999. *Freethinkers of Medieval Islam: Ibn al-Rāwandī, Abū Bakr al-Rāzī, and Their Impact on Islamic Thought*. Leiden: Brill.

Stroumsa, S. 2002. Review of D. De Smet, *Empedocles Arabus: Une lecture néoplatonicienne tardive*. Brussels, 1998. *Journal of the American Oriental Society* 122: 94–98.

Stroumsa, S. 2006. "Ibn Masarra and the Beginnings of Mystical Thought in al-Andalus." In *Mystical Approaches to God: Judaism, Christianity and Islam*, ed. P. Schäfer. Munich: Historisches Kolleg, Oldenbourg, 97–112.

Stroumsa, S. 2014. "The Muʿtazila in al-Andalus: The Footprints of a Phantom." *Journal of Intellectual History of the Islamicate World* 2: 80–100.

Stroumsa, S., and S. Sviri. 2009. "The Beginnings of Mystical Philosophy in al-Andalus: Ibn Masarra and His Epistle on Contemplation." *Jerusalem Studies in Arabic and Islam* 36: 201–53.

Sviri, S. 1996. "Spiritual Trends in Pre-Kabbalistic Judeo-Spanish Literature: The Case of Bahya Ibn Paqudah and Judah Halevi." *Donaire* 6: 78–84.

Thaʿālibī, al-. (*ʿUlūm*) 1317/1899–1900. *Al-ʿUlūm al-fākhira fī l-naẓar fī l-umūr al-ākhira*. Cairo: s.n.

Tornero, E. 1985. "Nota sobre el pensamiento de Abenmasarra." *Al-Qanṭara* 6: 503–6.

Tornero, E. 1993. "Noticia sobre la publicación de obras inéditas de Ibn Masarra." *Al-Qanṭara* 14: 47–64.

Van Ess, J. 1991–97. *Theologie und Gesellschaft im 2. und 3. Jahrhundert Hidschra: Eine Geschichte des religiösen Denkens im frühen Islam*. 6 vols. New York: de Gruyter.

Van Koningsveld, P.S. 1991. "Andalusian-Arabic Manuscripts from Medieval Christian Spain: Some Supplementary Notes". In M. Forstner (ed.), *Festgabe für Hans-Rudolf Singer zum 65 Geburtstage am 6 April überreicht von seinen Freunden und Kollegen*. Frankfurt a. M. and Bern: P. Lang. Vol. II, 811–23.

CHAPTER 5

AL-FĀRĀBĪ'S (D. 950) ON *THE ONE AND ONENESS*

Some Preliminary Remarks on Its Structure, Contents, and Theological Implications

DAMIEN JANOS

5.1. Introduction

Abū Naṣr Muḥammad al-Fārābī (d. 339/950) is regarded as one of the foremost Arabic philosophers of the early period of Islamic civilization. Born around 256/870 into a family that was originally from Transoxania, he acquired his philosophical formation in the company of Syriac Christian thinkers and eventually settled in Baghdad, where he contributed in various crucial ways to the development of a philosophical curriculum in Arabic. He also spent time in Syria and Egypt, where, as in the ʿAbbasid capital, he taught a younger generation of Syriac philosophers. Referred to as "The Second Teacher" in the Islamic tradition, he was held in high esteem in particular for his commentaries on Aristotle and his mastery of the *Organon*. Al-Fārābī wrote extensively on logic, physics, and metaphysics, reshaping much of the late-antique philosophical legacy into a system that was intelligible to the Arabic audience of his day and that addressed some of the pressing social and spiritual issues that prevailed during this period. He established a synthesis of various scientific and philosophical trends that bridged the theoretical and practical disciplines and redefined the place of human beings in the world by explaining political and religious phenomena in light of cosmological and epistemological theories.

Al-Fārābī wrote different types of works, which can be broadly classified as follows: (*a*) propaedeutic and methodological works providing instruction on the philosophical curriculum and its method, particularly on points of logic; (*b*) commentaries, mostly on Aristotle; (*c*) short treatises on various specific and technical subjects; (*d*) philosophical compendia covering various topics in a systematic and integrated way;

(*e*) polemical works, mostly in defense of Aristotelian tenets. Perhaps the most famous works of the Farabian corpus are the two philosophical compendia, *The Principles of the Opinions of the Inhabitants of the Virtuous City* (*Mabādiʾ ārāʾ ahl al-madīna al-fāḍila*) and *The Principles of the Existents* (*Mabādiʾ l-mawjūdāt*), also known as *The Political Regime* (*al-Siyāsa al-madaniyya*; I shall refer to them as al-Fārābī's "cosmological works" from now on), which cover a wide diversity of topics ranging from theology and cosmology to sublunary physics, psychology, and political theory.

The aim of the present chapter is to provide a preliminary analysis of some key features of a short and neglected treatise by al-Fārābī entitled *On the One and Oneness* (*Kitāb al-Wāḥid wa-l-waḥda*, henceforth *On the One*). In spite of its potential importance for our understanding of al-Fārābī's philosophy, this text has never been the object of a special analytical study and has been discussed only briefly and fleetingly in the secondary literature (see Walzer's comments in al-Fārābī, *Principles of the Opinions*, 339–42, 362; Vallat 2004, 64, 68, 79; Menn 2008, 91 n. 39; Menn 2012, 88–92; Janos 2012, 196–97; Rudolph 2012, 395, 430–31; Mushtak 1960 and Mahdi 1989 consist chiefly of an edition and/or translation of the text). There is therefore a strong desideratum to examine the style, structure, and contents of this work and to shed light on its relation to the rest of the Farabian corpus. This in turn would enable us to interpret its philosophical significance within the broader context of al-Fārābī's thought.

With this in mind, three questions in particular will orient the following study: (1) To what philosophical traditions and movements is this work indebted? (2) What are some of its main formal and doctrinal features? (3) And how do its contents fit in al-Fārābī's philosophical system? These are broad questions, and only preliminary insight can be provided here. Although short in length and technical in nature, *On the One* is at the same time representative of al-Fārābī's approach to philosophy and of his metaphysical program in particular. It deals with a topic of great importance to the Second Teacher, who, like many of his Greek forebears, tackled the issue of oneness and multiplicity in depth in his works. This neglected treatise may therefore serve as an entry point into some of the broader questions of his philosophy, while at the same time providing a glimpse into the state of contemporary research in Farabian studies.

5.2. General Presentation of the Work

Among the bio-bibliographers, Ibn al-Qifṭī (d. 646/1248) in *Taʾrīkh al-ḥukamāʾ* (279.9–10) and Ibn Abī Uṣaybiʿa (d. 668/1270) in *ʿUyūn al-anbāʾ* (139.8) both mention a *Kitāb al-Wāḥid wa-l-waḥda* in the long list of works by al-Fārābī that they provide. The work is furthermore cited by some later Arabic philosophers, including Ibn Bājja (d. 533/1138) and Averroes (d. 595/1198), and it is likely that Yaḥyā ibn ʿAdī (d. 974) and Avicenna (d. 427/1037) relied on it for their treatment of oneness in *The Discourse on Divine Unity* (*Maqāla fī l-tawḥīd*) and *The Cure* (*Kitāb al-Shifāʾ*) respectively, although they do not cite it directly. These authors take the Farabian authorship of this work for granted and